BEYOND 2020
KINGDOM AGE OF MATURITY
MICHAEL A. DANFORTH

Beyond 2020

DANFORTH MINISTRIES
MOUNTAIN TOP INTERNATIONAL
P.O. Box 43 Yakima, WA. 98907

The Kingdom Age Of Maturity

Beyond 2020
The Kingdom Age of Maturity

Danforth Ministries Publications

ISBN 978-0-9815944-0-8

Strong's Concordance with Greek and Hebrew Lexicon

All Quotes by Michael A. Danforth unless otherwise indicated.

All news quotes and information were copied by permission from online public resources. All science and technical information noted in this book can be viewed or researched on the Internet.

Wikipedia free encyclopedia, ***"wikipedia.org"***

Michael A. Danforth," ***Total Recall - Remembering The Original You" "Space The Prophetic Frontier" "Evolution of Another Kind"***

All interior images printed by permission – Fotolia.com or public Internet.

Cover Design by Craig Danforth

Editing and page layout by my sister-in-Love, Sheryl Jones and amazing wife, Tamera J. Danforth

For information regarding permission to reproduce material from this book, please email or write:

Address:
Michael A. or Tamera J. Danforth
Danforth Ministries / MTI
PO Box 43
Yakima, Washington 98907

Email:
Michael@mticenter.com Tamera@mticenter.com

Follow Michael A. Danforth at:

Website:
www.danforthministies.com

YouTube:
Michael Danforth

Facebook Page:
Danforth Ministries

Podcasts:
ITunes, Podomatic, Google, Spotify

In the light of the future, the contents of this book are unforgiving. Meaning, I cannot undo what I will write. While it may appear risky to some, I felt the Lord urging me to take a bigger step of faith and release what I believe to be the future heart and intentions of God for His people in 2020, and beyond.

Therefore, I do so from a place of co-creating with God. While my intent is not to minimize the prophetic mantle on my life, my higher hope and aim is to speak from the place of sonship. After all, is this not the primary goal of the Ekklesia to manifest the glory of Jesus Christ, through the revelation of sonship, (Which is both male and female)?

In terms of functioning as a prophet, thus creating future outcomes, I was recently reminded I am a ***"good news prophet."*** I am certainly not denying bad things don't happen and they will continue to happen, but on a limited scale. However my goal is not to highlight darkness, but to highlight God's increasing love and glory for all people and nations to see and know.

This is my quest:

To walk in the love of God, engaging in heaven and on Earth, for the purpose of seeing the kingdom of the world become the kingdom of God.
(Revelation 11:15)

Table of Contents

Prophetic Future Outcomes

These are just a few prophetic insights and foresights of the future expectations of heaven on Earth. Some of which, I will share in more detail in this book.

- The Love of God will be viewed as the ultimate judgment of heaven on Earth.
- Recently, I received a prophetic word from my sister-in love Sheryl, ***"You are a prophet of good news."*** I love it! In the future, prophets of **"*good news*"** will rise across the world.
- National media networks will eventually move from bad news to good news.
- The spirit of wisdom will become the future influence of heaven on Earth.
- Governments and groups who strongly oppose righteousness will implode. The standard of righteousness will continue to rise.
- The supernatural age of peace and rest will cover the Earth in unimaginable ways.
- Heaven is all about the light of the glory of the Lord. As a result, future technology will increasingly break the barrier of light. Every industry in the world will eventually be impacted by light. Every kingdom in the world will eventually come under the authority of light. Because God is light.
- The body of Christ will move from being warriors of conflict to warriors of love and peace.
- Signs and wonders will be redefined. This means tomorrow's supernatural displays of heaven on Earth, will appear off the charts of previous demonstrations.

- The captive will be set free in every nation, thus experience a newfound freedom through the power of God.
- Roe VS Wade will be overturned in the highest courts of the land. It will first appear as a mere trickle, from state to state, and then suddenly a floodgate of life will open up.
- Both Republican and Democratic parties will be redefined. We will first, see the imploding of the Democratic Party, then a total remake of the Republican. All of which, are only temporary orders until the order of heaven becomes more visible.
- Donald Trump will continue his presidency for another term. After which, God will promote an amazing woman into the highest office of the land. The fragrance of healing, peace and rest will be released over the land.
- The stock markets will take on a whole new look. What was once the driving force of the economy will be no more. The genius of God is rising upon the Earth, all of which has begun to redefine future economics.
- The future awakening of mankind will include the awakening of creation. This means the restraints of creation will increasingly be removed and a communication with all creation will emerge. All of which are designed to reveal the eternal attributes of God hidden within all creation.
- A revelation of ascension glory will cover the Earth in profound ways. At which time, the *"ascended ones"* will be revealed. The nature of the love and power of God working in them will exceed anything the Earth has ever seen.
- The atmospheres of heaven, including the thrones of God, will eventually create a merging of heaven and Earth, at which time,

glorious creatures will be seen for the very first time. Each will corporately release a knowledge and glory of God beyond belief.

- The laws of physics, including gravity, light and sound will be completely redefined. During this time of unveiling, what was once considered a limitation will be no more.
- Just as time serves those in heaven, so time will begin to serve God's people on Earth. In others words, time is coming under our feet.
- As humanity continues to be swallowed up by immortality, death and decay will visibly come under the power of sonship. As a result time will continue to slow down, and extended years of life will become the new norm.
- Many nations across the world will undergo a divine correction at which time every nation will experience a transformation of leadership, which will become an eventual gate of glory and divine partnership with other nations who are like-minded.
- The current sounds on Earth will eventually fade beneath new sounds from heaven. These sounds, frequencies and vibrations will break the barrier of humanity, which will exceed the limitation of hearing with our natural ears. Our spiritual senses will increase, our natural ability to hear sound from within, rather than from without.
- Destructive forces such as fires, earthquakes, volcanic eruptions, and storms of every kind; will eventually be harnessed by the sons and daughters of God. In addition, new technologies and inventions will become the new wave of dealing with natural disasters.

- Another star will be added to the Unites States flag. This word was in conjunction with another step of government being added to the White House, which is now known as, “Space Force.”
- Before President Trump’s presidency is over, the USA will be on the pathway of becoming debt free.
- Predicting future outcomes will fade beneath the kingdom age of co-creating with God.
- An endless supply of treasures will be harvested from space.
- The outer limits of space will transform into a new glorious display of the wonders and beauty of God.

The Kingdom Age Of Maturity

When thinking of *the "kingdom age of maturity"* it's important to think of it in terms of seeing the love, glory and power of God's kingdom reaching its fullest potential on the Earth.

Contrary to some belief, the kingdom of God is not a physical world of rules, feasts, food and drink, but instead a realm filled with love and the endless spiritual realities of God's divine nature.

"For the kingdom of God is not a matter of rules about food and drink, but is in the realm of the Holy Spirit, filled with righteousness, peace, and joy." (Romans 14:17 TPT)

From a natural perspective, it's hard to imagine the kingdom of God, and the kingdom of heaven living within us. All that is in heaven, in the kingdom of God, is in the people of God.

"Jesus was once asked by the Jewish religious leaders, "When will God's kingdom realm come?" (When will it be established?) Jesus responded, "God's kingdom realm does not come simply by obeying principles or by waiting for signs. The kingdom is not discovered in one place or another, for God's kingdom realm is

already expanding within some of you." (The realm of God's kingdom appears in us, through Jesus, by faith.)
(Luke 17:20-21 TPT)

Again, when speaking to the disciples about the kingdom of God, and how they should be praying, Jesus said,

"May your Kingdom come soon. May your will be done on earth, as it is in heaven."
(Matthew 6:10 NLT)

Jesus wasn't just telling them to pray for the kingdom of God to come, He was telling them to pray for the kingdom of God to become visible on the Earth at the same level of visibility in heaven.

With this in mind, loving God and others is at the epicenter of kingdom transformation. In conjunction, learning to co-create with God is also a huge key toward the restoration of all things.

Beyond 2020, an unimaginable gateway of the love and power of God will exponentially rise upon the Earth. To the degree the kingdom of God rises in us is the degree we can enter into our already resurrected state in Jesus Christ.

The kingdom age we are now living in demands we tune our spiritual senses to the frequencies and vibrations of God's love. This tuning process is the act of acclimating ourselves to the light of God in us, thus becoming the light of the world.

Some of the greatest obstacles to the advancement of God's kingdom become evident when we partner with the spirit of the world. This means partnering with its political, religious forms and rhetoric of the day. All of these and more, have the potential to pollute the minds of God's people; interfering with the purity of God's divine intent.

As a people in God, it's important to recognize we are spiraling up the mountain of the Lord into the revelation of our already ascended state in the kingdom of heaven.

In this royal place of glory and honor we realize the important task given to us is to create the future as joint heirs in Christ. This means, as sons and daughters of God, we are not just predicting future outcomes, but creating them according to the revelation knowledge of God's love and glory.

This age of God's kingdom consist of multiple layers of endless eternal revelation.

Each field of glory and revelatory insight into the Father's heart carries the potential to eternally alter our life and the world in endless ways.

The transformation of a new heaven and a new Earth is about the transformation of hearts and minds functioning as creative sons and daughters of God, thus creating future outcomes of heaven on Earth.

Some of you might be thinking: *"But what about the darkness? Shouldn't we be concerned or focused on all the acts of evil as well?"*

When it comes to darkness, John brings to light (no pun intended) a very important perspective:

"…The reason the Son of God was revealed was to undo and destroy the works of the devil." (1 John 3:8 TPT)

This means, we should not look at darkness from the perspective of increasing, but decreasing. The moment Jesus was born into the Earth the works of the enemy began to unravel, thus the eventual annihilation of all the works of the enemy.

Beyond 2020 will bring to light one very important truth, ***"The gates of hell will not prevail!"*** This holds true for any circumstance in your life.

Our heavenly mandate is to: ***"Set our minds on things above, not on things below."*** The Passion Translation describes it like this:

"Yes, feast on all the treasures of the heavenly realm and fill your thoughts with heavenly realities, and not with the distractions of the natural realm."
(Colossians 3:2 TPT)

The distractions of the natural realm are anything that tries to turn our focus away from our eternal ascended state in Jesus Christ.

Like most things in life, our perspective of the future and eternity, is dependent upon our ability to train our spiritual senses to perceive beyond the physical world.

"For every spiritual infant who lives on milk is not yet pierced by the revelation of righteousness. But solid food is for the mature, whose spiritual senses perceive heavenly matters. And they have been adequately trained by what they've experienced to emerge with understanding of the difference between what is truly excellent and what is evil and harmful."
(Hebrews 5:13-14 TPT)

I would like to simply point out a couple of truths:

"...Solid food is for the mature, whose spiritual senses Perceive heavenly matters..."

I want to announce to you:

The milk age of Christianity is quickly coming to a close.

Because of the increase of God's kingdom on Earth, many who are freshly entering into the revelation of the light of God are being catapulted into an extreme relationship with His love and glory.

Beyond 2020, the number of devoted lovers of God will exceed any other generation before us. Future signs and wonders will be off the charts of previous experiences. Kingdom revelation and understanding will reveal the mysteries of heaven in indescribable ways. The hidden attributes of God concealed in all creation will suddenly become visible for all to see. The restraints on creation now will eventually be completely removed.

The genius of heaven will appear in humanity beyond belief. A person's natural age will no longer be a consideration to measure the genius and wisdom of God in them. Children from all walks of life, like Jesus, will astound biblical scholars, scientists, artist and mathematicians. Most everything in this life that has appeared to reach its optimal peak will suddenly break the barrier of future belief or comprehension.

All the above, at one level or another is already present in the Earth. I recently read an article about a 12-year-old girl named, Lydia Sebastian.

September 11, 2015 in **Today.com,** read:

"Lydia Sebastian submitted an IQ test and achieved the top score of 162 on Mensa's Cattell III B paper, suggesting she has a higher IQ than well-known geniuses Albert Einstein and Stephen Hawking."

This is just one of many examples of how even the natural mind is being influenced by the brilliance of God. However, there's a supernatural knowledge, wisdom and understanding, blanketing the Earth beyond human comprehension.

In light of the climate of heaven increasing on Earth, we can no longer live in the halls of spiritual immaturity. As already mentioned, the age of spiritual immaturity is dramatically coming to a close.

Our ultimate source and foundation of growing up into the heart and mind of God will always be determined by our desire and ability to walk in the revelation of the Word and Love of God.

Anything less will fail to express the fullness of God's intended glory.

It is my hope the writings within this book will inspire you to reach your fullest potential in God and equip you to co-create with Father at the highest possible level. As you will soon discover, there is no end to the measure of God's love and glory, which is available to anyone who desires to know Him. Your access into the heart and mind of God has no end.

A Prophet's Reward

It was in the early 2000's when my brother Craig and I entered into a high school gymnasium in Portland, Oregon. Kim Clement, a well-known prophet who has since fully graduated to heaven, was holding a weekend prophetic gathering. To date, Kim is probably one of the most intense accurate prophets I have ever had the privilege of knowing. His ability to see into the future intent of God left a lasting impression in my life.

During this particular gathering, Kim suddenly stopped and looked toward the back of the auditorium where Craig and I were seated. He pointed to Craig and asked him to stand.

This is a brief excerpt of that prophetic word.

"You came into this meeting with a prophet, a true prophet of the Lord. I see you standing in front of two mountains. Be careful you choose the right one. One is a mountain of destiny; the other is a mountain of aimlessly searching for your purpose in God. The

mountain of destiny will lead you into great abundance, the other will lead you through a season of lack, but in the end, God will prove Himself faithful on your behalf. "

After the meeting, Craig was given a cassette of the prophecy spoken over him. Receiving a cassette tape gives you an idea of how far back this prophetic encounter was. On our drive home that night, we listened to the word again. As we listened, we both realized the "true prophet" he was referring to, was me. And, one of the mountains he was speaking of was ***"Mountain Top International"*** which was a ministry we formed a year earlier.

During that meeting, Kim preached about a future glory rising in the Earth. He spoke about a kingdom age of maturity, which would eventually reveal the sons and daughters of God.

As I set there listening to Kim's words about the future, it was as if a thousand arrows of eternal revelation pierced my heart. I could see the future, 2020 and beyond. I saw future gates of glory and revelation opening up on the inside of me. I saw the physical realm taking on an entire new look, its beauty and glory was beyond words.

In that moment, the sound of Kim's voice began to fade into the background of an unveiling glory rising up in my heart and mind. In the spirit, I began to move from one glorious future to the next.

Like blankets of liquid love, I watched the entire world being overlaid with one layer of glory after another. During that prophetic encounter, I heard the Spirit say:

"I'm inviting you come up here and stand on this mountain of future foresight and insight and co-create with me, a hopeful tomorrow. As you learn to co-create My intent and desire for My people, they too will be inspired to climb this heavenly mountain of love and glory. They will see for

themselves the amazing opportunities they have to create with Me; the future expectations of heaven on Earth."

Needless to say, that night, ***Mountain Top International*** took on an entire new meaning for me. I knew my life would never be the same.

The Mountain Of The Lord

Since its beginning *in 1998,* ***Mountain Top International*** has been privileged to partner with some amazing friends and family. You have literally been the backbone of our progression in the kingdom of God. We will forever be grateful for your endless love and generosity.

In reference to **Mountain Top**, one of my favorite spontaneous songs written by Kim Clement was a song titled, ***"The Mountain of The Lord."*** I first heard Kim sing this song at a prophetic gathering in New York City in 2008.

Here is a brief excerpt from the chorus of that song:

"In the mountain of the Lord I can hear your voice, in the mountain of Lord I can touch your face. There is a place for those who are thirsty in the mountain of the Lord..."

I love how the expression of this song speaks about being ***"in"*** the mountain of the Lord, rather than just ***"on"*** the mountain. *Daniel describes* *the giant statue (kingdoms of the world) in Nebuchadnezzar's dream, being struck down with the stone (Jesus), which became a great mountain (the kingdom of God) and filled the whole Earth.* ***(Daniel 2:35-45)***

This is the heavenly enthronement God is drawing His people into in this present age. Isaiah describes this kingdom mountain as the house of the Lord, into which all nations enter.

"Now it will come about that in the last days, the Mountain of the house of the Lord will be established as the chief of the mountains, and will be raised above the hills; and all the nations will stream to it." (Isaiah 2:2)

In 2020, and beyond the Lord will continue to build His house. This glorious house will eventually grow up into a mountain of glory, as prophesied by the prophet Isaiah.

This house of glory, which we are, will be the chief mountain of the Lord, which will reside over all the kingdoms and nations of the world. This same mountain is the holy tabernacle of Yahweh. The gravity of its love and glory will become so powerful all the nations of the world will be drawn up into its glorious light.

Some years ago, I was worshiping the Lord when I had a vision of myself standing on the mountain of the Lord. As I stood there, I saw a sea of people climbing up the same mountain I was standing on. At that moment, I was brought into another layer of Isaiah's vision when he saw all the nations of the world going up into the mountain of God, learning of His ways and walking on His paths.

"And many peoples will come and say, 'Come, let us go up to the mountain of the Lord, to the house of the God of Jacob; That He may teach us concerning His ways and that we may walk in His paths.' For the law will go forth from Zion and the word of the Lord from Jerusalem."

(Isaiah 2:3)

In this vision, I was holding a golden scepter in my hand, extending it out over the Earth. In my book, "***Space the Prophetic Frontier,***" I wrote about an open vision I had of an ancient one who showed me a golden scepter lying against a rock on top of a mountain.

He said: ***"The scepter is in the high place."***

So here I was, standing on the mountain of the Lord extending that same scepter of authority over the Earth.

As I continued to worship, I realized, in the spirit, King David was standing by my side with the harp of heaven in his hands.

It was then when I discovered the instruments in our hands, my guitar and David's harp, in concert with the sound of our voice, were the golden scepters of authority given to us in the high places of God. I instinctively knew this kingdom sound was being released for the purpose of co-creating with Father.

As we continued to move in the spontaneity of the Spirit, I sensed an eternal mergence of heaven and Earth coming together as one. The sound of glory coming out of me merged perfectly with the sound of heaven. I then heard a harmonious sound of creative authority being released over the nations of the world. As the agreement of heaven and Earth intensified, an increasing number of people began to climb up the mountain of the Lord.

"Beyond 2020, a new sound will rise upon the Earth, lifting up nations into the mystical creative realms of God's glory."

As the sound of God continued to vibrate through my entire being, I heard the Lord say:

"You asked me if you could have this mountain and I said, yes!"

I suddenly realized how ***Mountain Top International*** came into being. It was as though the name and eternal intent of ***MTI*** had always been living inside of me, just waiting for its time to be born into the Earth.

I remember feeling completely overwhelmed by the approval of heaven over my life. It was as if God was saying, *"I approved your purpose and destiny in Me before the foundations of the world."*

This means, you and I were born with the *"Yes"* of God in our hearts.

"Beyond 2020, we will witness a major transformation in the spirit of prophecy."

John writes*:*

"...The testimony of Jesus is the Spirit of prophecy."
(Revelation 19:10)

This means prophecy is the essence or fragrance of Jesus.

Right now, the people of God are being invited to climb into the mountain of the Lord, which is a glorious picture of stepping into Jesus Christ.

As a result, the entire world will witness tribes and nations melting into the hot fervent love of the Father's heart.

Creators Of Heaven And Earth

Beyond 2020 will display our ability as co-creators with God. This amazing opportunity to create with God includes all the tenses of time: past, present and future.

Before I share some great testimonies of how God has used me to participate in the aligning of Earth with heaven, I would like to first give you a brief foundational perspective of where I am coming from.

The first time I realized God was inviting me to co-create the future, thus override death and decay, dates back as far as the early 2000's. Through prayer, praise and worship, I was invited to see creation from the perspective of heaven.

Of course, at the time, I didn't know God was inviting me to literally override the physical decay of Earth with the glory of heaven. At least, not to the degree I know now.

What I initially thought to be just some random prophetic experiences eventually turned into a deeper understanding of God's divine intent. Some of which, I have already shared in previous books. Nonetheless, it took me a few years to acclimate my heart and mind into this extended revelation of the *"restoration of all things."*

Even though I did not know it at the time, God was leading me out of a prophetic mindset of just predicting the future, into creating it.

Whenever we speak about creating heaven on Earth, we must see it through the lenses of God's love invading Earth as in heaven. In this sense, we are called to override death with life. Though Jesus, through His death and resurrection, disarmed powers and principalities of the air, He is still waiting for His people to rise up into the **revelation of the completed work of the cross.**

Through the revelation of sonship, we are afforded the opportunity to supernaturally co-create the future intentions of Father, beyond Earth. All the emptiness of space, planets and galaxies are future canvases waiting for the creative glory of the sons of God.

As a result, the office of the prophet is still undergoing a major transformation. The primary function of the *"five-fold"* ministry is to equip the people of God into the maturation of Jesus Christ, thus the revelation of being sons and daughters of God.
In reference to the function of apostles, prophets, evangelists, pastors and teachers, Paul writes:

> ***"These grace ministries will function until we all attain oneness in the faith, until we all experience the fullness of what it means to know the Son of God, and finally we become one perfect man, with the full dimensions of spiritual maturity and fully developed in the abundance of Christ."***
> ***(Ephesians 4:13 TPT)***

All of the above point to a moment in time when the body of Christ will grow up into the revelation of what it means to live in the perfected love of Jesus. At which time, all the dimensions or expressions of the government of God's love and power will be fully expressed in all creation.

As I've already stated, the function of a prophet is moving from a mere predictor of future events, to supernaturally co-creating with the eternal intentions of Father on Earth. We must not forget the expansion of God's kingdom on Earth is directly related to the expansion of His kingdom in Heaven.

So what does this look like in real time? What does it mean to co-create with God?

Before we can create or release the divine intentions of heaven on Earth, it's important we know what the intentions of God are for His people.

John quotes Jesus as saying:

"A thief has only one thing in mind, he wants to steal, slaughter, and destroy. But I have come to give you everything in abundance, more than you expect; life in its fullness until you overflow!"
(John 10:10 TPT)

Wow! What a contrast to the destructive language that has filtered into the hearts and minds of the body of Christ. Many see God as a punisher of people for the sake of law and order. If that were the case, in light of all the recent senseless murders of men and women across the world, I would have to say God is doing a poor job in keeping them in line. My point is this; *we are the divine intervention of heaven on Earth.*

However, the bible does say, God disciplines or reproves those He loves:

"...My son, do not regard lightly the discipline of the Lord, nor faint when you are reproved by Him; for those whom the Lord loves He disciplines, and He scourges every son whom He receives."
Hebrews 12:5-6)

I love how the Passion Translation reads:

"...My child, don't underestimate the value of the discipline and training of the Lord God, or get depressed when he has to correct you. For the Lord's training of your life is the evidence of his faithful love. And when he draws you to himself, it proves you are his delightful child."
(Hebrews 12:5-6 TPT)

As you can see, there's a huge difference between correcting, training or reproving a child you love, versus, punishing them or condemning them to death for the sake of obedience.

I love how John describes Jesus's heart:

"God did not send his Son into the world to judge and condemn the world, but to be its Savior and rescue it!"
(John 3:17 TPT)

"Beyond 2020 will reveal the sons and daughters of God moving from just a *'rescuing'* perspective into a *'reigning perception'* of glory."

In keeping with ***(John 10:10)*** Jesus makes it very clear the enemy has one primary goal, which is to completely annihilate humanity from the face of the Earth.

On the other hand, Jesus also makes His intentions very clear:

"I've come to give you everything...in abundance, even more than you would ever expect, think, or imagine. I've come to give you life in its entirety, until you cannot contain it anymore."

What! Come on God!

As if that's not convincing enough, John quotes Jesus again as saying:

"The Holy Spirit is the one who gives life, that which is

of the natural realm is of no help. The words I speak to you are Spirit and life..." (John 6:63 TPT)

Wow! The glorious power of the breath of God, in us, is literally off the charts of heavenly intent.

Modern Day Scribes

Another powerful example of co-creating the past, present and future is through the function of a scribe. I believe this chapter will offer you a gateway to enter into a deeper revelation of your scribal anointing in the kingdom of God.

As we cross over the threshold beyond 2020, we will witness a generation of scribes rising in the Earth, greater than any other time.

As the body of Christ moves deeper into the revelation of what it means to be a scribal son or daughter of God, an unusual agreement of heaven will appear on the Earth at a magnitude the world has never witnessed.

This is not some hypothetical gesture of a hopeful outcome, this is unwavering belief a future generation of modern day scribes will sweep across the Earth. They will have profound insight and foresight of the Father's heart for all people.

Vision Of Heavenly Scribes

In July of 2017, I found myself in the spirit. Standing in front of me were three men, each holding a staff in their hands. As I looked at them, I instinctively knew by the spirit one of them was Ezra. Prior to this encounter, I really didn't know much about Ezra except he was a priest and scribe in early biblical times.

During this experience, I heard the Lord say, ***"In heaven you are a scribe."*** I have to admit; when I first heard these words I was somewhat disappointed. The idea of writing for eternity seemed borderline depressing. I thought, *"What would I write about that heaven doesn't already know?"* That thought no sooner flashed through my mind when I heard the Lord say:

"My kingdom is an ever expanding kingdom, and to it, there is no end."

I was instantly overcome by a floodgate of knowledge flowing through me. The download was so intense; it was impossible for me to separate one understanding from another.

And then, it was over.

There I sat. Holding my guitar in my lap, with my arms resting on its edge, contemplating the reality of what I had just experienced.

A few days later, while making preparations for an upcoming meeting, I came across a scripture in Judges:

"From Ephraim those whose root is in Amalek came down, following you, Benjamin, with your peoples; from Machir commanders came down, and from Zebulun those who wield the staff (reed) of office (scribe)."
(Judges 5:14)

In ancient biblical times, pens were made from reeds.

John writes:

"I had many things to write to you, but I am not willing to write them to you with pen (reed) and ink..." (3 John 1:13)

The writers in Hezekiah's age were all too familiar with two classes of writing. One was with a reed on paper and skin, and the other with an iron tool with the point of a diamond.

Jeremiah writes:

"The sin of Judah is written with a pen of iron, and with the point of a diamond: it is graven upon the table of their heart..." (Jeremiah 17:1)

I later found other scriptures and Hebraic perspectives that fully supported the idea of a staff or rod being referenced to the authority of the pen of a scribe.

As you can imagine, my scribal encounter suddenly took on a whole new meaning. I realized the staffs I saw in the hands of the three men represented *pens of authority*.

Sometime later I was reminded of what the Lord said to me, ***"In heaven you are a scribe."*** He wasn't saying, *"After you die and go to heaven, you will be a scribe."* He was saying, *right now, in heaven, you are a scribe."*

I was struck with the awesome reality of functioning as a modern day scribe, even greater still, the opportunity to co-create with heaven on Earth.

This means, my current scribal mantle on Earth is merely a prerequisite for how I will create future outcomes, and yes, even new worlds. I realize for some this sounds too extreme, but for others, it resonates in your heart and spirit.

The pen of a modern day scribe virtually has no limitations as to what it can release upon the Earth, and in heaven.

These Kingdom scribes consist of writers of books, poets, songs, painters, decrees, executive orders of government at the highest levels, deeds of property, and any other actions that release or articulate kingdom authority. There is really no limit to the scribal authority given to us for the purpose of walking in the abundance and authority of God.

I believe all the above, at one level or another has the potential to be recorded as signatures of agreement, thus placed in the archives of heaven as a testimony of the expansion of God's kingdom.

Just as we can receive knowledge of things pertinent for Earth, so we can receive knowledge of things that pertain to heaven.

As modern day scribes, we are relationally positioned to see and hear the intent of heaven, and then transfer that same treasure of intent upon the Earth.

"Jesus said to them, "Therefore every scribe who has become a disciple of the Kingdom of heaven is like a head of a household, who brings out of his treasure things new and old."
(Matthew 13:52)

Another translation reads:

"He responded, "Every scholar of the Scriptures, who is instructed in the ways of heaven's kingdom realm, is like a wealthy home owner with his house filled with treasures both new and old. And he knows how and when to bring them out to show others."
(Matthew 13:52 TPT)

You might be thinking, **"I do not consider myself a scribe or scholar of the word."**

The word *"scholar"* is defined as: *"A person who is highly educated or has an aptitude for study, or attends a school or studies under a teacher. It also refers to a person who has pursued advanced studies in a specific field."* (**Merriam Weber Dictionary**)

Everyone is called to be a scholar of the word of God. At one level or another we all have the responsibility to know the word of God.

In speaking to Timothy, Paul writes:

> ***"Always be eager to present yourself before God as a perfect and mature minister, without shame, as one who correctly explains the Word of Truth."***
> ***(2 Timothy 2:15 TPT)***

The word ***"eager"*** refers to someone taking the word of God serious enough to search it out for themselves. This single step of intent can put you on the pathway of becoming a scholar of God's word.

I believe God has appointed scribes in every kingdom of the world. Whether you're specialty is agriculture, education, science, entertainment, business, or a domestic mom or dad, you have the potential to become a modern day scribe of heaven on Earth.

The Prophet Ezra

If you recall, in my scribal vision I told you I recognized one of the scribes as Ezra. I have since learned the prophet Ezra was one of the first real known *"soferims"* of early biblical days. He was an important administrator connected with the Temple, but without religious status.

According to the Bible, Ezra recovered a copy of the Torah (Genesis, Exodus, Leviticus, Numbers, and Deuteronomy) and read it aloud to the whole nation. From that moment on, the Jewish scribes solidified the following process for creating copies of the Torah and eventually other books in the Old Testament. As a result, the soferim and their tradition of biblical scholarship were eventually largely taken over by the Pharisees.

Historically, whenever kings of ancient times or any other ruler wanted to know about the laws or decrees of the land, they would ask the scribes, who watched over all the written documents of the land.

It wasn't until around 2nd century BC, the soferim eventually disappeared. Later, New Testament references to scribes, who were often connected to the Pharisees, became the eventual doctors of the law.

Scribal Restoration

I believe we are currently in a time when heavenly scribes are being restored back to their governmental authority in the Kingdom of God.

As already mentioned, these modern day scribes come from all walks of life, each inherently carrying a record of the original intent of God for His people.

Throughout history we can see how God emphasized the importance of keeping record of all that was spoken and witnessed. Without written record of the actions of God toward humanity, we wouldn't have access to what we now call, "The Bible, "the inspired word of God.

Every time you write down something you believe to be inspired by the Spirit of God, angels know if that word truly is a revelation from heaven. If it is, they are assigned to that word for the purpose of seeing it fulfilled in the manner God desires. This includes any authoritative scribal function at every level in life.

Over the years, I have increasingly discovered how to co-create the purpose and intent of God on Earth, and in heaven. Again, this means, I'm not just predicting future outcomes, but creating them through the unction of the Spirit.

Unfortunately, the ability to create future chaos and death through prophetic writings and verbal decrees, are also all too common in the Christian world. Nonetheless, a divine correction is now in play.

One of the primary reasons I started writing books, was because the Lord instructed me to keep track of everything He would tell me or show me about the future. At the time, I didn't fully understand He was inviting me to co-create with Him.

Eventually, my book writing became a by-product of keeping record of the intent and desire of God for His people. Unlike verbal declarations, documented prophetic writings or decrees create a greater accountability.

Write It Down

I want to leave you with one final emphasis and experience on this subject of functioning as a modern day scribe.

First, one of the most important things to remember is, ***"Write it down!"*** When you write down what you believe God is saying, at the very least, it proves you value His words.

I view all technological advancements as part of an important process for keeping record of the intentions of God for His people. So if I say, ***"write it down"*** I am also saying, ***"record it!"*** Whatever process you choose is up to you. Every time you write or record something the Father wants to release upon the Earth, you position yourself to partner with God on behalf of the people of God.

In the book of Habakkuk we read:

"I will stand on my guard post and station myself on the rampart; and I will keep watch to see what He will speak to me, and how I may reply when I am reproved. Then the Lord answered me and said, "Record the vision and inscribe it on tablets that the one who reads it may run." "For the vision is yet for the appointed time; It hastens (eager to get there) toward the goal and it will not fail (not lie). Though it tarries, wait for it; for it will certainly come, it will not delay." (Habakkuk 2:1-3)

Wow! Come on! Are you catching this? Habakkuk is waiting on the rampart, which is in reference to a place of view at the top of a castle wall. It depicts a seer of God waiting on the Lord.

After God speaks to him and shows him what is to come, He first instructs Habakkuk to ***record the vision.*** In other words, picture the future outcome in your heart and mind.

Then God instructs him to write it down so others can see the intent of God and run with the message. This isn't just in reference to people running with the word of God, but angels as well. When the angels of the Lord see what's been recorded, they know whether it's God. Again, they run with it and carry out its divine intent. In Revelation we read:

"Now I want you to write what you have seen, what is, and what will be after the things that I reveal to you." (Revelation 1:19 TPT)

This is another great example of the importance of documenting any divine inspiration, idea, dream or vision. In this instant, John was instructed to write down what he saw in the past, present and future. As a result, he was able to scribe the intentions of God beyond all limitations.

The Government Of Israel

In keeping with the understanding of a modern day scribe, I want to share one of the ways God afforded me the opportunity to co-create the future government of Israel. I'm not implying I was the only one, but I was certainly within the rank of influence.

During the first few months of 2019, there were high doubts as to the reelection of Prime Minister Benjamin Netanyahu. As many of you know (like many national elections) there were a lot of alarming accusations against Israel's Prime Minister. During the height of what appeared to be a very difficult race, I was lifted up into an eternal perspective of God's intentions toward Israel. This means, I was lifted outside the intent and influences of the world and was brought into the intent and influences of heaven.

I was then prompt to set down and prophetically declare the intentions of God toward the nation of Israel, which I posted on many social media outlets.

Here are a few of the prophetic posts I released on the eve of March 22, 2019.

"Israel will prevail! God did not bring Israel this far into His future intent, only to see the future government of Israel interrupted by the evil demise of the enemy. The government of God will continue to increase over the land in ways most never imagined."

"A supernatural gateway has opened! We are co-creators with God! We have been seated in the theater of heaven for such a time as this."

And again, on March 23, 2019, I posted:

"Since 2016, I have boldly declared, 'no more war!' Many believe this to be a hopeful dream at best. However, I believe an unusual shift of government across the world is about to reveal the divine intent of Father at an epic level. I also have a sense the future shift in leadership in Israel is equally destined to favor the intent of God toward an eventual supernatural gateway into peace and unity. Come on God!"

On April10, 2019, **Israeli News Networks** declared:

"Israeli PM Benjamin Netanyahu Wins Record Fifth Term In Office!"

Wow! There is nothing more gratifying than functioning as an eternal gateway of heaven.

Like John in the book of Revelation, we must hear the call of God to ***"Come up"*** into His future plans for all nations. Until such time, we will always fall short of the ability to co-create with God at the level He desires. Let me encourage you to lift up your head and behold the treasure of heaven, and become a doorway for this glorious treasure to be realized in your life and in the nations of the world.

"For I am confident of this very thing, that He who began a good work in you will perfect it until the day of Christ Jesus."
(Philippians 1:6)

It's important to note the *"day of Jesus Christ"* is not just some projected date in the future, but it's here and now. The *"day"* is in reference to the light of God's glory.

"For God, who said, "Light shall shine out of darkness," is the One who has shone in our hearts to give the Light of the knowledge of the glory of God in the face of Christ."
(2 Corinthians 4:6)

The gates of heaven are open now! They are waiting to be accessed in ways most never anticipated!

Jesus spoke to Nathanael and said:

"...Truly, truly, I say to you, you will see the heavens opened and the angels of God ascending and descending on the Son of Man."
(John 1:51)

Dead Sea Comes To Life

In the early 2000's, my daughter Amber, another friend and myself went to Europe, Israel and Africa all in one collective journey.

During our visit to Israel, one of our many stops included visiting the Dead Sea. We were looking forward to floating the salty waters of buoyancy.

For those of you who might not know, the high salinity in the Dead Sea increases the density of the water, which in turn, makes objects in the water more buoyant. All you have to do in the Dead Sea is simply recline and just float. In fact, it's hard to swim because of the buoyancy of the water.

After our time of fun and relaxation, we stood on the shores of the Dead Sea, taking one last look at its unusual existence.

In that brief moment of reflection, the Spirit of God suddenly came over me. I lifted my arms toward the Dead Sea and invited everyone to join me.

I began to prophesy life over the waters. I rebuked the salty sea of death and commanded the waters to come back to life. Later at a special gathering, I shared our experience of the Dead Sea and declared:

"A day would come when the Dead Sea would be known as the Sea of Life."

I spoke how this seemingly impossible event would be a sign the power of restoration would become more evident in Israel, and the world, at a level never witnessed.

On October 4, 2018, **"Breaking Israel News"** reported:

"Ezekiel's End-of- Days Vison Revealed: Dead Sea Coming to Life."

A brief excerpt from this news report reads:

"Recently, scientists have been shocked to discover that the sinkholes appearing around the sea are quickly filling up with fish and other forms of life previously unseen in the inhospitable region."

Many Hebraic scholars believe this is the fulfillment of the prophet Ezekiel's prophecy:

"...And there will be very many fish, for these waters there, and others, will become fresh; so everything will live where the river goes. And it will come about that fishermen will stand beside it; from Engedi to Eneglaim there will be a place for the spreading of nets. Their fish will be according to their kinds, like the fish of the Great Sea, very many." (Ezekiel 47:9-10)

This is just a small glimpse into our present and future potential in God to release the breath of life over all creation.

Because of the love of God living in us, *"the words we speak are Spirit they are life."*

I pray you hear this; we have been invited by Father to co-create from heaven on Earth beyond any other generation before us.

"Beyond 2020, you can expect to see all creation align itself to the increasing power of restoration flowing through the sons and daughters of God."

In addition, I believe this is huge indicator of dreams and visions many thought were dead suddenly coming back to life.

The age of barrenness is over! This might remind you of former prophetic words, but there is something about the fruitfulness of God coming through the people of God exceeding any other generation before us. For the sake of not repeating myself in a future chapter of this book, I will leave you with this thought of kingdom encouragement and future expectancy,

"The season of opportunity you thought had come and gone is still in you, waiting to be birthed through the faith of God working in you."

2020 VISION

In keeping with the subject of co-creating with God, it's important to see Beyond 2020, and through the eyes of increasing glory. From this glorious perspective we are able to see into the eternal government of heaven, thus again, releasing that same government of love and power on the Earth.

In 2004, at a public gathering, in Yakima, Washington, I prophetically declared, **"The dividing wall between church and state is coming down."** Mind you, given the current declination of the United States government at the time, this prophetic declaration appeared very unlikely.

In the early 2000's, these kinds of prophetic gatherings were very common for us. Through praise and worship we would ascend into the heavenly courts of heaven and align ourselves with the purposes of God, expecting what we heard and saw to come to pass.

In 2012, ***Mountain Top International*** held another conference at the Yakima Convention Center. We invited multiple musicians and singers from all over to join us. Like many of our other gatherings, our purpose was to prophetically come into agreement with heaven and release the future expectations of Father for His people.

During this particular conference in 2012, I once again prophesied *about "the dividing wall between church and state coming down."* In the spirit, I could see dividing walls literally crumbling to the ground. Again, by faith, we celebrated this historic governmental moment.

Now, fast forward to 2017 and 2018, where multiple US Media Outlets are declaring:

"The White House Is Tearing Down the Wall Between Church and State."

One of the statements read:

"President Trump in a Rose Garden ceremony Thursday signed an executive order removing the wall between Church and State."

Another report read:

"Attorney General Jeff Sessions reads out of the book of Romans creating an historic stage for an unimaginable moment."

Come on! You don't have to be a prophet or prophetess in order to co-create the future intent of heaven on Earth. God is looking for sons and daughters who can hear from heaven and see with supernatural 2020 vision.

Increasingly over the years, I have personally witnessed more and more people, not just hearing the voice of God, but also seeing and experiencing the glory of God face-to-face.
As a result, the Ekklesia of God is now breaking the 2020 threshold of sight.

Most are familiar with the term "20/20 vision." It's a term used to express normal visual acuity (the clarity or sharpness of vision) measured at a distance of 20 feet. If you have 20/100 vision it means you must be as close as 20 feet to see what a person with normal **vision** can see at 100 feet.

Supernaturally speaking, 20/20 vision affords us the ability to see the future intentions of God a great distance away with greater clarity. This supernatural vision affords us the insight and foresight to see into the heart of God up-close and personal, while at the same time seeing the expected future landscape of heaven on Earth.

As we break the 2020 threshold of time our ability to see by the Spirit of God will exponentially move off the charts of former probabilities.

Over the centuries an untold number of people have been blinded by the illusions of darkness. On the other hand, countless others are coming into the light. They are beginning to see into the incredible revelation of God's love. As a result, they are piercing the darkness with the light of God's love in indescribable ways.

We should never settle for just hearing the voice of God, but seeing the glory of God face-to-face.

"But God still loved us with such great love. He is so rich in compassion and mercy. Even when we were dead and doomed in our many sins, he united us into the very life of Christ and saved us by his wonderful grace! He raised us up with Christ the exalted One, and we ascended with him into the glorious perfection and authority of the heavenly realm, for we are now co-seated as one with Christ! Throughout the coming ages will be the visible display of the infinite, limitless riches of his grace and kindness, which was showered upon us in Jesus Christ." (Ephesians 2:4-7 TPT)

As you can see, being seated in heaven means we have supernaturally ascended ***"Into the glorious perfection and authority in the heavenly realm."*** Other translations read: ***"realms."***

I believe this is a more accurate description of heaven. A great analogy is Earth consisting of cities, states and countries. Likewise, heaven consists of multiple realms that express the glory of God in endless ways.

In Acts we read:

"...for in Him we live and move and exist..."
(Acts 17:28)

Living ***in*** Christ affords us the ability to see heaven and Earth from the inside out (in the heart of God) not just the outside in. It's the difference of having revelation of truth versus actually experiencing truth and walking in that truth in real time.

I remember hearing Bill Johnson (senior leader at Bethel in Redding, Calif.) say:

"Too often we settle for just the revelation of truth, rather than moving into the actual experience of truth." B.J.

"We are presently being invited to see God, experience God, and not just hear God. " M.D.

There are multiple ways to see God. One primary way is through the actions of God's love toward His people.

These actions work in us and through us. These same actions include, but are not limited to: *acts of love, kindness, a giving heart, signs, wonders and miracles.* All these and more enable the world to see and experience God's love. But most of all, showing love for one another is one of greatest ways to demonstrate the love of God.

"For when you demonstrate the same love I have for you by loving one another, everyone will know that you're my true followers."
(John 13:35 TPT)

All of the above and more are important steps to encountering God face-to-face.

Even after Moses had experienced some of the most amazing signs and wonders ever displayed upon the Earth, he still asked:

"Show me your glory."

Beyond 2020, God will reveal the face of His love to such extreme that people and nations will come into His light seemingly in a day.

If Moses could be invited to break through the veil of obscurity, how much can we who are in Christ, ***"walk in the light as He is in the light."***

"For now we see but a faint reflection of riddles and mysteries as though reflected in a mirror, but one day we will see face-to-face. My understanding is incomplete now, but one day I will understand everything, just as everything about me has been fully understood." (1 Corinthians 13:12 TPT)

I want to suggest to you, as sons and daughters of God, in Christ, we have moved beyond the veil of obscurity and are now afforded the opportunity to see the love and glory of God face-to-face. Just as Father knows everything about you and I, so He longs for us to know Him.

Like John we are continually being called up into the eternal realms of glory to discover our full inheritance in the kingdom of God.

So, here we are, standing at the threshold of witnessing another historic supernatural unveiling of God's face. Soon we will realize, we are already like Him.

"Beloved, now we are children of God, and it has not appeared as yet what we will be. We know that when He appears, we will be like Him, because we will see Him just as He is." (1 John 3:2)

The Merging Of Time

I think time has gotten a bad rap. Because of death and decay, time has been viewed as a negative, rather than a positive. From the perspective of eternity, time was never intended to be a rule of limitation, but a means to express the endless glory and power of God.

"Beyond 2020, we will become increasing aware of time coming under our feet."

This means, rather than us serving time, time is beginning to serve us. Contrary to popular belief, heaven is not absent of time. However, in heaven, time serves the purposes of God, not the other way around. In this sense, God is outside of time, because He is the source and beginning of time.

Using time and distance as a force to expand the kingdom of God is a wonderful thing. Time in the hands of God, is like a giant rubber band being stretched to whatever length desired to manifest His glory.

Supernatural imagination, revelation, teleportation, and any other supernatural means of traveling through time and space, will eventually override all the tenses of time, (past, present and future) which are presently subject to the increasing life of God in us.

On September 20, 2015, I prophetically declared these words:

"Have you noticed? Time is changing. It is increasing, not decreasing. Once again, eternity is knocking at the door. Time as you know it will never be the same again. Its decayed state is fading away. Watch as the zones of time merge. The two shall become one."

Over the last couple of years, there has been a lot of discussion about getting rid of ***"daylight saving time."*** In November 2018, California voted to end DST.

One national media group reported:

"In addition to releasing us from the burden of having to reset our clocks twice a year, this will also reduce the number of time zones in the United States from four to two."

On March 11, 2019, President Trump tweeted:

"Making Daylight Saving Time permanent is O.K. with me!"

Again, I don't view this prophetic word as a mere prediction of some future event about time, but a co-creating the eternal intentions of heaven on Earth.

Presently, this 100-year-old tradition of saving time, which was initially instigated during World War I, is not only on the chopping block in the United States, but in other parts of the world as well.

DST is used in over 70 countries worldwide and affects over 1 billion people every year. The beginning and end dates vary from one country to another.

I believe all of this, points to a time (no pun intend) when time as we know it, will never be viewed the same again.

The Transformation of Time

Something extraordinary is happening to the physical world of time. Time is merging into a singularity of the past, present and future. In this sense, multiple time zones are becoming one. Just as our mortal state is being consumed by immortality, physical time is being consumed by eternity.

Prior to sin entering into the world there was only one time zone called eternity, but within eternity times and seasons still existed.

After sin entered through the portal of humanity it produced its own time. Now we have time in heaven and time on Earth.

However, ultimately there can only be one time. This supernatural realm of time called "eternity" is rapidly swallowing up the temporal state of all creation.

Lifted Up Into Eternal Time

Through Jesus Christ, we have been lifted up reinstated (seated in heavenly places) into the eternal time zone of heaven. As the love of God increases in His people, time on Earth will continue to come under the influence of eternity.

When the disciples asked Jesus how they should pray, Jesus said pray: ***"...Your kingdom come, Your will be done on Earth as in heaven..."*** This divine intent of heaven on Earth is an unstoppable reality. As the kingdom of God increases on the Earth, it continues to push out death and decay, which are properties of temporal time.

"As the limits on time decrease, the age of God's people will increase."

Recently, a scientist named **Aubrey de Grey**, who studies regenerative medicine, reported:

"New biotechnology will let people who are already alive today reach the ripe old age of 1,000 years." Come on God!

Of course, most scientists mock at the idea of mankind living beyond 150 years, let alone a 1000.

The prophet Isaiah quotes God as saying:

"For Behold, I create new heavens and a new earth; and the former things will not be remembered or come to mind..."
(Isaiah 65:17)

"...No longer will people be considered old at one hundred. Only the curse (cursed mentality) will die that young."
(Isaiah 65:20 NLT)

If you think, *"this is crazy!"* I agree! It is absolutely crazily probable!

"...All things are possible to him who believes."
(Mark 9:23)

All of the above are largely outside the scope of earthly possibilities. Our only hope for seeing and embracing this kind of kingdom reality is through our eternal inheritance in Jesus Christ.

"The illusion of time and space is getting thinner and thinner."

Beyond 2020, the idea of being caught up into the third heaven will no longer be a goal for the people of God to achieve. Why? Because the merging of heaven with Earth will become so apparent, the illusion of separation between the two will simply disappear.

In reference to the coming of Jesus, Matthew quotes John as saying:

"The realm of heaven's kingdom is about to appear— so you'd better keep turning away from evil and turn back to God!" (Matthew 3:2 TPT)

John was preparing the way for the coming Christ. He was introducing the coming of God's kingdom upon the Earth. The moment Jesus arrived we went from an introduction of the kingdom of God, to ***"the kingdom of God is here."*** Now, the kingdom of God is all around us, in us, and upon us. But the fullness of that kingdom has not yet manifested to the degree it is known in heaven.

Therefore the position of heaven has nothing to do with being up there somewhere in the unknown cosmos.

It's about the authority and power of God's love and glory being highly expressed through us.

Thunder And Lightning

"From the throne came flashes of lightning and the rumble of thunder. And in front of the throne were seven torches with burning flames. This is the sevenfold Spirit of God."
(Revelation 4:5 NLT)

On July 17, 2012, at another prophetic gathering, I experienced the thunder and lightning of God. In the spirit, I impulsively reached out and grabbed hold of the lightning rods coming from the throne of God. I started bending them toward specific areas of government worldwide, including the United States. As I watched the lightning rods of God strike governmental thrones across the world, the thundering sounds were deafening.

Shortly thereafter, within 24 hours of this throne room encounter, our city, and the entire Pacific Northwest, experienced a thunder and lightning storm. It thundered so loudly it literally shattered the windows of a couple of businesses in our downtown area.

Multiple areas across the Pacific Northwest, including Seattle, Washington were struck with historic bolts of lightning.

Years later, beginning in 2016, we began to witness some of the most intense governmental exposures of our time. The exposures of governmental corruption, just in the United States alone, have been off the charts.

Even the most recent exposure of governmental corruption in the United States, will pale to what is about to happen in 2020, and beyond.

The Dethronement Of Corrupt Rulers

I believe 2020; will mark another historic period of an extended dethronement of corrupt government on a level the world has never seen.

At which time, the spirit of reformation and restoration will become increasingly more evident.

We should never underestimate the restorative power of God's love. Even though God's intent is to expose the darkest intentions of humanity, it is for the purpose of leading these same people into a place of love, healing and restoration.

God is not out to destroy humanity, but to draw them into the revelation of His love.

The Apostle Paul writes:

"But all things become visible when they are exposed by the light. For everything that becomes visible is light." For this reason it says, "Awake, sleeper, and arise from the dead, and Christ will shine on you."
(Ephesians 5:13-14)

Many people think light shining in the darkness is for the purpose of getting rid of divisive people who have been acting contrary toward the intentions of God. However, I believe the most harden of hearts are destined to become the greatest influences of light the world has ever seen.

Paul writes:

"...Everything that becomes visible is light."

In other words, everything that comes out of the clutches of darkness potentially becomes the light of God. What a beautiful picture of hope for those separated from the light of God's love.

The future is not only hopeful, but off the charts in terms of a glorious people reaching the highest mark possible in the kingdom of God.

From an eternal perspective, we started in the love of God and we will end in an overwhelming revelation of that same love.

While I'm certainly not naïve to the future challenges this world has in store for us. I am extremely confident in our ability and faith in God to overcome them all. Thus exhibit a level of sonship and kingdom authority never experienced.

"For God so loved the world that He gave His only begotten Son..."
(John 3:16)

And He will continue to pour out that same love over and over.

For years, God has been speaking to me about an unusual graduation of the physical world and its eventual transformation.

Beyond 2020 will mark the tipping point when we will begin to see the restorative power of God's love, impacting the entire world at incredible levels. At which time, a supernatural awakening will become apparent, not just in humanity, but in all of creation.

The Great Exposure

There are three major ways I see darkness being minimized in the world, which I perceive all as an intervention of God's love. The first is through **"light exposing the darkness,** which is the action of light shining in the darkness.

The ultimate destruction of darkness, thus the work of the enemy, is through the power of God's love.

Beginning in August 11, 2012 thru April 27, 2014, I repeatedly released the following prophetic word now known as, ***"The Great Exposure."***

"The next historical unveiling has begun. I know to some I must sound like a broken record when I tell you once again, the great exposure is now upon the governments of this nation (United States) and other nations in the world.

Another veil is being ripped away and will reveal a shocking revelation of what has been going on behind the closed doors of

government. These include leaders in the church, technology, entertainment, science, education and politics. All these and more are just the beginning of a global exposure. Many have believed the evil opposing the intentions of God has gone unchecked. These same people also believe it is the final demise toward an event called 'the end times.

However, in the near future, you will see how wrong this perception really is. God is not slack toward the works of evil. The next level of unveiling of these evil works has already begun and its self-inflicting judgment will be realized.

On the other side of this coming great exposure lies the unveiling of the glory of heaven on Earth in ways few ever dreamed possible."

Since 2012, I have referenced this word numerous times. The initial recorded version of this particular prophecy can be heard on our website, ***danfortministries.com***, titled *"The great exposure."*

In a later chapter titled ***"Global Governmental Shifts,"*** I will unpack in more detail the ways in which these governmental shifts will appear, especially in the world of social media.

In 2012, I remember seeing explosions of light, like stars erupting in space, spreading over the darkest regions of the world. It reminded me of someone shooting a flare into the night sky. In that moment, I saw every evil form of corruption being exposed by the light of God. It was extremely beautiful and disturbing at the same time.

Presently, in the United States, an historic unveiling of corrupt government is quickly coming to light. This unveiling knows no boundaries, which means the government of the Church is equally postured to experience the intensity of God's light shining in the darkness.

As for the USA, regardless of what you might think of President Trump, he is undoubtedly anointed to expose the swamp of corruption, not only in the United States, but also in other nations of the world.

In August of 2012, I prophetically declared:

"God is bringing a leader to the forefront of the United States, one that cannot be bought or sold. He will be a man that knows how to add and subtract. He will take this nation out of the red into the black. Many will say *"We never saw this coming."*

After the election of President Trump, multiple news networks publicly responded with these words:

"No one ever saw this coming."

It's important to note, when it came to prophetically co-creating the future presidential election of 2016, in my opinion, no one said it with more accuracy and detail, in advance, than Kim Clement. As I already mentioned, I will forever be indebted to his relentless desire and boldness to align his heart with heaven on Earth.

I've always believed once someone releases the future intent of God into the atmosphere, it quickly becomes accessible to all who are connecting with the Spirit of God. Sometimes all it takes is single individuals to align themselves with the heart of God in order for heaven to kiss Earth.

There will always be those who run ahead of the present hour, blazing trails for the kingdom of God to invade the kingdoms of the world.

The degree of influence of any spiritual trailblazer in the kingdom of God is determined by his or her relationship with the Father. Intimacy, integrity and discipline will always govern the longevity of the gifts and callings of God flowing through His people.

Light Swallowing Darkness

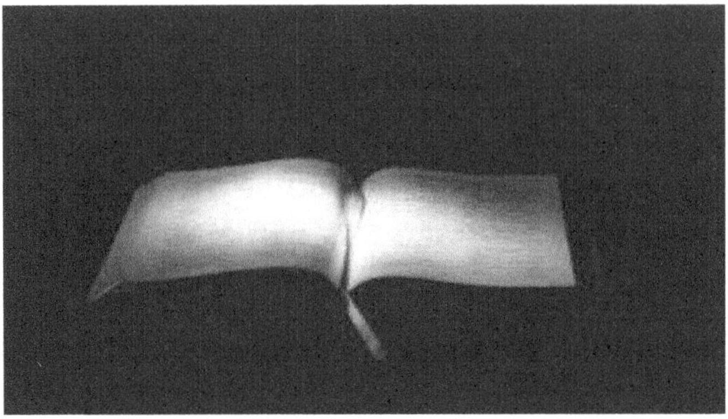

The second way I see darkness continually be minimized is through "**light swallowing up darkness.**" While darkness and light seem to be racing toward increasing maturity, no matter how dark, darkness may seem, it will always be swallowed up by the light of God's glory.

"For behold, darkness will cover the earth and deep darkness the peoples; But the Lord will rise upon you And His glory will appear upon you."
(Isaiah 60:2)

I see this as prophetic revelation of the coming Christ, thus the increasing glory of God's kingdom. In an age when darkness looked like a prevailing force on the Earth, manifesting itself through the heart of humanity, Isaiah could see a glory that would eventually swallowed up by the coming messiah, Jesus Christ. Since that day, the glory of God's kingdom has continued to override all the works of the enemy. ***(John 3:16, Luke 10:19)***

Without an eternal perspective of the future intent of God, it's impossible to really know the future potential of that same glorious light covering the Earth.

You can be assured, on its best day, darkness will never come near the magnitude of influence the love and glory of God is currently having in the hearts of humanity.

In my previous book, ***"Evolution of Another Kind"*** *I* described how future darkness will increasingly become backdrops to revealing God's glory:

"For the Scripture says to Pharaoh, For this very purpose I raised you up, to demonstrate My power in you, and that My name might be proclaimed throughout the whole earth."
(Romans 9:17)

Beyond 2020, I believe the world will cross over a new threshold into seeing the love and glory of God appearing in the darkest regions of the world on historic levels.

As a result, this same eternal glory will supernaturally manifest in and through people's lives in ways the world never expected.

Since the year 2000, I have repeatedly declared:

"The darkest regions of the world will become the future fields of God's glory."

Iran, Syria, Venezuela and North Korea, just to name a few, are destined to be fully invaded by the light of God's love. It's happening now.

Recently, a church in Iran was recognized as the fastest Christian growing church in the world. What? Yes, it's true.

In October 4, 2016, ***"Church Leaders News"*** reported:

"Iranian church is the fastest growing in the world."

On August 15, 2017, **CBN Network** notes:

"Iran's intelligence minister admitted publicly for the first time "Christianity is rapidly spreading throughout Iran."

It's hard for most to imagine the light of God's love is invading one of the darkest countries in the world at such an accelerated rate.

"The Light shines in the darkness, and the darkness did not comprehend (overpower) it."
(John 1:5)

The word *"comprehend"* also means, *"to contain."* Meaning, darkness will never be able to contain or overpower the kingdom of God's love. Don't ever give into the illusion darkness is increasing. It is nothing more than a failed attempt to bring you into agreement with death rather than life.

"In 2020, and beyond, what most viewed, as impenetrable walls of darkness, will seemingly crumble to the ground in a day."

History bears record the darkest works of the enemy are nothing more than an illusion of defeat. Throughout the ages, from Moses to Jesus, from the first apostles and disciples until now, all have left their overcoming footprint on the Earth.

We are on a pathway to witnessing the glory of God blanketing the Earth in undreamed-of ways.

The prophet Habakkuk describes 2020, and beyond like this:

"For the earth will be filled with the knowledge of the glory of the Lord, as the waters cover the sea."
(Habakkuk 2:14)

We also can read where the prophet Isaiah addresses a defining moment in Israel's early beginnings. I believe these same scriptures equally declare a prophetic proclamation for this day.

"Arise, Jerusalem! Let your light shine for all to see, for the glory of the Lord rises to shine on you. Darkness as black as night

covers all the nations of the earth, but the glory of the Lord rises and appears over you."
(Isaiah 60:1-2 NLT)

Once again, we can see the power and glory of God's love rising above the darkness, shinning its light into the deepest crevices of the human heart.

This is a picture of death being swallowed up by the light of God's glory. Let there be no doubt ***"the latter house of glory will be greater than the former."***

"The future glory of this Temple will be greater than its past glory, says the Lord of Heaven's Armies. And in this place I will bring peace. I, the Lord of Heaven's Armies, have spoken!"
(Haggai 2:9 NLT)

Again, no matter how intense darkness may appear, in and beyond 2020, the light of God's love will shine so brightly every dark intention will be cut down with the power of God's love, the sword of truth, the shield of faith and the supernatural gospel of peace.

"...The Son of God appeared for this purpose, to destroy the works of the devil."
(1 John 3:8)

The Implosion Of Darkness

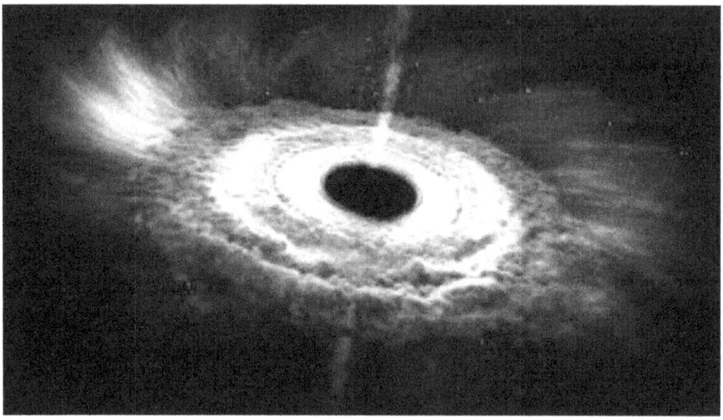

The third action to overriding darkness is through *"darkness imploding or caving in on itself."*

"Beyond 2020, we will witness the implosion of all kinds of evil."

"Implosion" is defined as: *"An instance of something collapsing violently inward. It also refers to a sudden failure or collapse of an organization or system."* (**Merriam-Webster Dictionary**)

The act of implosion plays a key role in the gravitational collapse of large stars. As a result, these implosions can lead to the creation of a supernova, neutron star or black hole. It presents the death of one thing that has the potential to give life to another.

This leads me to believe; on the heels of future implosions is the potential of the beginning of new life.

Over the last few years, I have repeatedly spoken about the implosion of government, in the United States, and the world. I declared:

"The walls of division will not stand, and like the walls of Jericho, they will eventually come tumbling down."

In August 5, 2019, an article was released by the **"American Thinker,"** which is a known national news publication in the United States.

The headlines read:

"The Democrat's Implosion"

A brief excerpt from that same article also reads:

"Looking back on the first 100 days of 2019, the year's biggest story by far has been the astonishing implosion of the Democratic Party."

You are mistaken if you assume this word is only directed toward a left wing party. This prophetic word is in reference to any organization bent on trying to obstruct the righteousness of God, even the political sphere of the Church.

As already mentioned, in 2012, I released several prophetic words about future government that have already come to pass. One of which describes the implosion of the R*epublican and Democratic parties.*

While this might sound shocking to some, it's a reminder the current governments in this nation and the world are a mere tutor to the government of God's kingdom, which is a government of love, peace, joy and unity. A divided house or government will never stand the test of time.

"Now, Jesus supernaturally perceived their thoughts and motives, so he confronted them by telling them this parable: "Any kingdom that fights against itself will end up in ruins. And any family or community splintered by strife will fall apart." (Matthew 12:25 TPT)

For the sake of fulfilling the purposes of God, all the above is a small indicator of a much larger implosion about to sweep across the Earth.

We are now standing on a threshold when governments, businesses, international networks, and anything else that has given itself over to a depraved mind, will seemingly collapse overnight. All of these and more will soon discover they cannot escape the light of God.

"The future implosions of evil will no longer dominate the media networks of the world."

I think it's important to point out the majority of these exposures will be the result of a *self-destructive behavior.*

Many people in the church always seem to default toward *"God is bringing judgment upon the land."* I see this as a spiritual copout. The fact is implosions are the result of our own actions or choices in life. Even then, God is still continually running interference hoping we will come into the revelation of His amazing love.

We should always be careful not to come into agreement with death, but with life.

"Future godless implosions are the result of evil becoming victim to its own demise."

Again, I do not interpret this as some angry judgment being released upon people and nations, rather a bold declaration of the light of God turning over rocks, exposing what's underneath.

In light of all the corruption going on in the world, I believe God has relentlessly appealed to the hearts of countless people who have been bent on working against Him, rather than for Him.

In the future, many like Saul, who later became the apostle Paul, will be converted by the revelation of God's love; becoming extreme advocates for righteousness.

Nonetheless, those who refuse to yield to the divine intentions of God will be released over to their own decayed mentality; known as: ***"A depraved mind."***

Paul describes this kind of depravity like this:

"And because they thought it was worthless to embrace the true knowledge of God, God gave them over to a worthless (depraved) mind-set, to break all rules of proper conduct. Their sinful lives became full of every kind of evil, wicked schemes, greed, and cruelty. Their hearts overflowed with jealous cravings, and with conflict and strife, which drove them into hateful arguments and murder. They are deceitful liars full of hostility. They are gossips who love to spread malicious slander. With inflated egos they hurl hateful insults at God, yet they are nothing more than arrogant boasters. They are rebels against their parents and totally immoral. They are senseless, faithless, ruthless, heartless, and completely merciless. Although they are fully aware of God's laws and proper order, and knowing that those who do all of these things deserve to die, yet they still go headlong into darkness, encouraging others to do the same and applauding them when they do!

(Romans 1:28-32 TPT)

Prior to the scriptures of above, Paul points out the sexual depravity between men and women and their unnatural lust and desire for each other. However, this isn't just about sexual depravity, but any depravity contrary to the divine nature of God for His people. Even though they were aware their choices were worthy of death, they still chose to run toward darkness with a determination to take as many as they could with them, all the while applauding others who were mimicking their same evil actions.

God giving them over to a depraved mind-set is a picture of self-implosion.

Unfortunately, this extreme example of depravity pales in light of some of the darker appetites being expressed today.

As I already stated in an earlier chapter:

"We should never underestimate the restorative power of God's love. Even though God's intent is to expose the darkest intentions of humanity, it is for the purpose of leading these same people into a place of love, healing and restoration."

In this chapter you will be challenged to see outside another traditional box of kingdom thinking. We are crossing the threshold into an unusual display of signs and wonders, which will redefine our perspective and interaction with all creation.

We are presently living in a kingdom age of transformation, which will present creation in a light we have never seen.

On the morning of April 16, 2019, during my morning routine, I heard the Lord say:

"Space is waking up."

I then heard:

"Because My love and glory are increasing in My people, all creation is beginning to wake up, even in the outer limits of space."

My heart leapt with immense joy and great anticipation! It felt as though I was about to witness something that would announce another layer of awakening glory on Earth and in the heavens above.

For those of you, who might find this a bit unnerving; let me give you some brief history on how I arrived to this point of expected enthusiasm.

In 2010, I wrote a book titled ***"Space the Prophetic Frontier."*** I spoke about a time in the future when all creation would begin to wake up, not only to our sonship in the kingdom of God, but to creation's fuller potential. I have long anticipated a point in the future when creation would release its high praises; beyond it's current reductive natural state.

David declared:

"Praise Him, sun and moon; Praise Him, all stars of light! Praise Him. Praise him highest heavens, and the waters that are above the heavens! Let them praise the name of the Lord, for He commanded and they were created."
(Psalms 148:3-5)

Even as I write this now, I can see every restraint coming off, which was implemented through sin, death, and decay. We are in the age of the *restoration of all things* spoken by Peter in the book of Acts:

"...and that He may send Jesus, the Christ appointed for you, whom heaven must receive until the period of restoration of all things about which God spoke by the mouth of His holy prophets from ancient time."
(Acts 3:20-21)

As a result of all the above, like David, for years I have been prophesying over creation to awaken to its true state in the kingdom of God. And like David, I have been releasing the song of the Lord knowing the day would come when creation would begin to wake up.

I have long been privileged to be a part of some amazing responses of creation toward the glory of sonship in me.

A day after the Lord spoke these words to me on an early March morning; I came across a national news report that read:

"A strange sleeping magnetar just "Woke Up" after a decade of silence." (Science New March 18, 2019)

What? No way! 2020, is destined to unveil a global awakening, racing across the universe.

"This is the age when creation will release new songs and praises unto the Lord."

Eternal songs will increasingly be heard from the outer limits of space. It's time for the people to declare, *"Wake up! Wake up! For the glory of the Lord is upon you now!"*

The increasing light and love of God is leading His people out of a sleeping slumber.

"...Awake, sleeper, and arise from the dead, and Christ will shine on you." (Ephesians 5:14)

It's time to awaken the dreams and visions God has given you and prophetically declare:

"The dreams and visions of God in me have not died and are awakening to the purpose and destiny of God in me."

The Celebration of Sonship

A few years ago, on an early winter morning, I was setting in my car in an empty parking lot. I often like to take an early morning drive before the city wakes up.

On this particular morning, with coffee in hand and music playing, I begin to set my heart and mind on the heavenlies and all it's glorious wonder. It's an excellent way for me to calibrate my senses toward the love of God and His divine intentions.

As I entered into this moment of deep meditation, my eyes focused on some trees planted in the mediums of the parking lot in front of me. Suddenly, the limbs of the trees began to slightly sway back and forth. I assumed it was because of the blowing of the wind. I watched, as the leafless branches started moving more aggressively, clapping together as if they were applauding the morning sun rising over the Eastern mountains of the valley.

I rolled down my window thinking I would take in some of the cool winter breeze, but to my surprise there was no breeze, none whatsoever. Yet, the trees in front of me continued to sway.

As I steadied my gaze on the leafless motion of the trees, beautiful colored leaves started to appear on barren branches.

I thought, *"What is this? This can't be real."* In that same moment, I heard the Lord say:

"Creation is applauding your ability to see its true eternal state in the kingdom of heaven. It's celebrating the glory of sonship."

"Wow! How amazing is that!"

This passage of scripture came to mind:

"For you will go out with joy and be led forth with peace;
The mountains and the hills will break forth into shouts of joy before you, and all the trees of the field will clap their hands."
(Isaiah 55:12)

As we move beyond the 2020 barrier, another layer of the joy of the Lord will increasingly rise on the Earth. Instead of fear, the supernatural peace and love of God will become the apparent glory in His people.

All of creation will increasingly celebrate the glory of God in ways the world has never witnessed. It will appear as though a ***Narnia*** moment has come upon the Earth.

All of this represents another level of spiritual maturity rising in the Earth, stirring all creation toward a heighten awareness of the love and glory of God. It's another profound indicator death and decay are coming under our feet.

As we increasingly see creation from the perspective of eternity, which is its true eternal nature, the spirit of mourning will completely dissipate from all creation.

"The age of mourning for the glory of the Lord is being silenced by the brightness of His coming." ***For the anxious longing of the creation waits eagerly for the revealing of the sons of God." (Romans 8:19)***

This means, the once anxious longing of creation is shifting from a state of mourning into a state of kingdom celebration.

Partnering With Creation

I realize this kind of glorious awakening sounds like a fairy tale experience full of exaggerated imagination. I am confident; sooner or later you will become convinced of this unusual invasion of heaven on Earth.

Currently, Father is inviting His sons and daughters to partner with Him in awakening creation to it fullest state of kingdom glory.

"The entire universe is standing on tiptoe, yearning to see the unveiling of God's glorious sons and daughters! For against its will the universe itself has had to endure the empty futility, resulting from the consequences of human sin. But now, with eager expectation, all creation longs for freedom from its slavery to decay and to experience with us the wonderful freedom coming to God's children." (Romans 8:19-21 TPT)

This reminds me of children standing on their tiptoes, desperately longing to see the glory of those destined to unlock their fullest potential in the kingdom of God.

Beyond 2020, we will see the eager expectations of all creation being fulfilled. Who would have ever thought creation, like humanity, was subjected to slavery and decay, and now longs to experience eternal freedom with the children of God. As you will discover in the next chapter, this glorious revelation of universal freedom, takes *"setting the captives free"* to a whole new level.

All creation has purpose and was created to reveal the attributes of God. This means the entire universe plays an important role of revealing the glory of heaven on Earth.

"For ever since the world was created, people have seen the earth and sky. Through everything God made, they can clearly see his invisible qualities—his eternal power and divine nature. So they have no excuse for not knowing God."
(Romans 1:20 NLT)

It's difficult for many to imagine, just like the people of God are destined to go from glory to glory, so creation is moving from one realm of glory to the next. Each glorious stage of transformation is purposed to reveal the mysteries of heaven on Earth.

Divine Creative Interaction

St Francis Assisi lived from the year 1181 or 1182 to October 3 , 1226 is for many people the most Christ-like Christian of all ages. He gave up his fortune to live among the creatures of the land. On a daily basis, St Francis would preach to the birds and other animals. He respected nature and regarded all creatures as his brothers and sisters. It was said, all creatures would communicate the mysteries of God to him.

History also records him as having the ability to interact with God's creatures on a level none have ever witnessed before. Many witnesses say, "St Francis would dialogue with creation as though they were all part of the universal language of God's kingdom."

The future awakening of creation, like in the time of St Francis, will require personal interaction with the people of God. Humanity interacting with creation dates back as far as the first man and woman in the Garden of Eden. Even after the introduction of sin into the world, there were moments where the Bible highlighted unusual events with man and beast.

Around the year 2005, I released an article and publicly prophesied about a generation of sons and daughters who would enter into a *"Pakaw"* moment in history.

This revelation was inspired through the story of the prophet Balaam and his donkey. Balaam was on his way to hook up with the Moabites, which angered the Lord. As a result, God sent an angel to take Balaam out. However, Balaam's donkey could see the Angel with sword in hand and tried to go around him. Thus the moment of divine intervention escalated into a personal interaction between Balaam and his donkey.

"The angel of the Lord went further, and stood in a narrow place where there was no way to turn to the right hand or the left. When the donkey saw the angel of the Lord, she lay down under Balaam; so Balaam was angry and struck the donkey with his stick. And the Lord opened the mouth of the donkey, and she said to Balaam, "What have I done to you, that you have struck me these three times?" Then Balaam said to the donkey, "Because you have made a mockery of me! If there had been a sword in my hand, I would have killed you by now." The donkey said to Balaam, "Am I not your donkey on which you have ridden all your life to this day? Have I ever been accustomed to do so to you?" And he said, "No."
(Numbers 22:26-30)

The word *"open"* in reference to opening the donkey's mouth, comes from the Hebrew word *"Pakaw"* which means *"to loosen or remove restraint."* In other words, God removed the restraint of speech from the donkey, enabling him to openly communicate with Balaam. It's important to note scripture doesn't describe Balaam as being shocked at the donkey's ability to speak. In fact, he immediately began to engage with the donkey as if it were some family affair.

This leads me to believe prophets of old were acquainted with the ability to interact with creation beyond modern day understanding. This falls in line with earlier prophets understanding of taking authority over all creation.

In reference to speaking with creation, God speaks to Job saying:

"Just ask the animals and they will teach you. Ask the birds of the sky, and they will tell you. Speak to the Earth, and it will instruct you. Let the fish in the sea speak to you."
(Job 12:7-8 NLT)

Beyond 2020 we will witness a global *"Pakaw"* moment when countless people will establish a communicative relationship with creation on an historic level. At which time, a supernatural awakening will appear on the Earth, one of which will demonstrate the ability of all creation to manifest the glory of God beyond measure.

In the last couple of years, I have become more aware my knowledge of future weather patterns has not only come via the sound of God voice, but through the sound of creation as well. It's as though my spiritual ears are being tuned to the language and frequency of creation. As a result, I feel I am being kept in the loop concerning the future intent of God for all things. The simplicity is being still and listening to the language of heaven resonating through all creation.

I realize the idea of communicating with creation and actually expecting a response is beyond most human reasoning. However, this kingdom understanding reaches beyond the flesh, into the Spirit of God, through which all things were created by and for.

"For by Him all things were created, both in the heavens and on earth, visible and invisible, whether thrones or dominions or rulers or authorities—all things have been created through Him and for Him."
(Colossians 1:16)

Since all things were made by Him and for Him, and since we are in Christ, there is no reason we cannot know or communicate with creation at the same level Jesus does. All the above is part of our mystical inheritance in the kingdom of God.

Beyond 2020, all of this will become common practice among the people of God. At which time, a generation of men and women will exhibit their ability to personally interact with creation beyond comprehension.

Creation Knows The Voice Of Sonship

Josiah Said in the sight of Israel:

"...O sun, stand still at Gibeon, And O moon in the valley of Aijalon." So the sun stood still, and the moon stopped, until the nation avenged themselves of their enemies. Is it not written in the book of Jashar? And the sun stopped in the middle of the sky and did not hasten to go down for about a whole day."
(Joshua 10:12-13)

On October 30, 2017, the ***"Breaking Israel News"*** reported:

"Cambridge researchers announced Monday that they have pinpointed the date of the biblical account of Joshua stopping the sun — which they claim is the day of the oldest eclipse ever recorded — to October 30, 1207 BCE, exactly 3,224 years ago."

When we begin to interact with creation at the level of sonship every residue of any former curse will completely be removed. Like Joshua and others in his day, creation will respond to the voice of God; the voice of sonship in you.

Let me encourage you to lean into the sounds of heaven and prepare your heart to witness unfathomable acts of the kingdom of God. A curtain of manifested glory is being pulled back right now for the entire world to see and know the glory of heaven.

The Hebrew meaning and value for the number **2020** *"hatstsalah"* is *"deliverance."*

For several years now, I have prophetically spoken about the captive being set free. These acts of freedom encompass countless people worldwide. A supernatural display of divine deliverance is about to sweep across the Earth in untold measures.

Human trafficking at every level is being dealt a severe blow. These victims of horrific acts of evil will be rescued in mindboggling proportions.

Currently, sex trafficking is a multi-billion dollar global industry, and the Internet has enabled it to become one of the fastest growing illegal businesses in the world.

Because of privacy laws and technology that enables people to obscure their identities and locations, online human trafficking and sexual exploitation is extremely difficult to track.

However, advocates for these precious souls are increasing every day. As a result, a holy vengeance is being implemented on the Earth.

"In 2020, and beyond, we will witness the crumbling of human trafficking at levels the world has never encountered."

Even as I write this:

"The gift of knowledge is increasingly playing a key role in exposing these evil lairs of death. Through dreams and visions the perverted acts of darkness are being exposed to the light. Many who were thought to be dead will seemingly rise up out of the ashes of death and decay and become some of the greatest righteous liberators the world has ever known. "

Young men and women will come from the four corners of the Earth bearing testimony of their supernatural deliverance. They will do great exploits beyond comprehension. Their relentless love and compassion to set the captive free will shatter the halls of death and decay on historic levels.

In addition, entire families who have been sentenced to die in other countries for coming against the grossness of corrupt government will soon celebrate a newfound freedom.

Iran, North Korea, Syria, Venezuela and other nations in the world, who have senselessly imprisoned their own people for not conforming to their evil ways, will suddenly be overcome from the inside out. (Implosion)

Countless people within these nations will rise up with a holy vengeance and the power of God will be demonstrated mightily on their behalf.

The entire world will quickly realize the blood of the captive will not be silenced. Their longing to see life springing up in the shadows of death will become an eventual vengeance of heaven on Earth.

These are but a few examples of a greater scale of freedom about to sweep across the darkest regions of humanity.

Beyond 2020, you will see the age of evil regimes crumble to the ground and be scattered like dust.

"Therefore I say to you, the kingdom of God will be taken away from you and given to a people (nation) producing the fruit of it. And he who falls on this stone will be broken to pieces; but on whomever it falls, it will scatter him like dust."
(Matthew 21:43-44)

This increasing age of setting the captive free will make the deliverance of Israel seem like kids play. I am in no way minimizing the historical value of the deliverance of the Israelite people, but in terms of numbers, the future deliverances of God's people will be in the billions and trillions.

Some biblical scholars believe the number of captives set free by Moses during Pharaoh's rule was in the thousands, while others believe it was more like 2 million or more. Whatever the number may have been, it will still pale in comparison to what is to come.

Currently, all the above is being orchestrated from heavenly places. These heavenly courts of justice are being occupied with sons and daughters who have learned to access these chambers of glory, affording them the opportunity to co-create with Father on behalf of all those who long to be free.

Let there be no doubt in 2020, and beyond, the trumpeting ***age of deliverance*** will echo through the land, thus becoming a part of the last and final ***"great awakening."***

In 2017, Josh Baldwin released a song titled, "The War Is Over." The beginning lyrics of that song read:

"The war is over turn around, lay your weapons on the ground. The smoke is fading before the lie; the dead are coming back to life. He has made a way for us, born from glory out of dust. Children held within the arms of peace. He has made a way for all, mercy waits where sinners fall, He is our victory."

"The war is over His love has come, to call us daughters and sons. No longer orphans without a home, now we have found where we belong."

"Beyond 2020, we will witness the body of Christ coming out of a war mentality into "It is finished! The victory is already won!"

On October 9, 2009, I was in my office on an early Friday morning preparing for a conference about to start that evening. My norm is a quiet time of meditation, then picking up my guitar for a time of worship.

Before long, I found myself being overwhelmed by an intense presence and sound of holiness coming from what I perceived to be the throne of God. Even though I could not see them, I knew it was the sound of the living creatures circling the throne.

I then saw an endless rainbow of colors, which began to circle around me. Before I had a chance to determine if what I was seeing was real, all the colors suddenly went right through me. I was instantly filled with the knowledge of the Lord.

To say I was on overload would be a huge understatement. I remember feeling a strong wind swirling around me, which filled me with an acute awareness of the love of God. I heard a loud voice declare, "The War Is Over!"

Then I heard a knocking at my office door. It was the musicians arriving early to prepare for the evening meeting.

During that season in my life, the worship at ***Mountain Top International*** was very warring. We were always pulling down strongholds or breaking through the gates of heaven, as if armored with the sword of the Lord and war paint on our faces.

Just as we were beginning to engage in corporate worship, I could hear the words of the Lord again, echoing in my ears, ***"The war is over!"***

Suddenly I was gripped with an unusual presence of the peace and rest of God. My body felt as light as air. I thought, *"This is the wind of God I had just experienced earlier that day."* Now, I didn't have a care in the world; every burden had been lifted off of me.

From this place of peace and rest we began to worship the Lord. We were all gripped with a holy ecstasy of peace and love. The affection of God for His people poured through me. All we could do was drink from the fountain of glory, from this eternal river of life flowing through us. I knew then with great certainty, ***the war was over.***

This is not saying I don't have conflict in life, but I've been set free from a conflicting mindset. I now stand against the works of the enemy from a place of peace and rest. This is the revelation of being seated, resting, in heavenly places in Christ Jesus.

Beyond 2020, we will witness a kingdom age of maturity, of the rest and peace of God. Right now, I am beginning to hear more and more people declare, ***"No more war!"***

The triumphing revelation of David taking down Goliath was with the realization the battle belonged to the Lord.

This day the Lord will deliver you up into my hands, and I will strike you down and remove your head from you. And I will give the dead bodies of the army of the Philistines this day to the birds of the sky and the wild beasts of the earth, that all the earth may know that there is a God in Israel, and that all this assembly may know that the Lord does not deliver by sword or by spear; for the battle is the Lord's and He will give you into our hands."
(1 Samuel 17:46-47)

This is the same David, who later declared:

"The Lord is my shepherd, I shall not want. He makes me lie down n green pastures; He leads me beside still waters. He restores my soul; He guides me in the paths of righteousness For His name's sake..."
(Psalms 23:1-3)

The Age Of Rest And Peace

In keeping with the understanding of ***"no more war"*** I want to go beyond 2020, into the future age of *"rest and peace."* I am of the mind the love of God comes to us to lead us into this supernatural realm of rest and peace. As you will discover, this kingdom realm of expectation is at the center of God's heart for all humanity.

Outside of God's rest, we will continue down this tiring pathway of fighting the enemy at every turn.

Living in a mindset of being in constant war is not a New Covenant perspective of God's intent for His people.

God is love. This means the primary intentions and responses of God are highly motivated by love.

God's love is the foundational pathway to entering His rest. As a result, we are brought into the experience of the rest and peace of God working in our lives.

The testimony of Moses declares:

"Now therefore, I pray You, if I have found favor in Your sight, let me know Your ways that I may know You, so that I may find favor in Your sight. Consider too, that this nation is Your people." And He said, "My presence shall go with you, and I will give you rest." (Exodus 33:13-14)

Here we can see the favor of God, the presence of God, and the rest of God, working hand in hand.

"Beyond 2020, we will see the sons and daughters of God unveil a future hope that will strip away any ancient mantle that has tried to imprison the people of God into a mind of death and decay."

The perspective of darkness overtaking the Earth is a lie born out of a spirit of religion. The constant image of good versus evil has long been at the epicenter of Hollywood's intent. As a result, billions of people walk away with the knowledge that good and evil are, and will always be part of the interwoven fabric of every society.

This ancient idea of chaos, death and condemnation, which once had glory, has no glory today. Which means it is no longer part of the future equation of heaven on Earth.

"For if the former ministry of condemnation was ushered in with a measure of glory, how much more does the ministry that imparts righteousness far excel in glory. What once was glorious no longer holds any glory because of the increasingly greater glory that has replaced it. The fading ministry came with a portion of glory, but now we embrace the unfading ministry of a permanent impartation of glory." (2 Corinthians 3:9-11 TPT)

After appointing Moses to set Israel free, God made His intentions very clear:

"Then I will take you for My people, and I will be your God; and you shall know that I am the Lord your God, who brought you out from under the burdens of the Egyptians."* *(Exodus 6:7)

Currently, there are billions of people who find it difficult to imagine ever coming out from under the worrying burdens of life.

Jesus declared:

"Are you weary, carrying a heavy burden? Then come to me. I will refresh your life, for I am your oasis. Simply join your life with mine. Learn my ways and you'll discover that I'm gentle, humble, easy to please. You will find refreshment and rest in me. For all that I require of you will be pleasant and easy to bear."* *(Matthew 11:28-30)

I know this is hard for some to believe, but in 2020, we will begin to see the weight of bearing the burdens of life reach an all-time low. Come on God!

Living in the rest of God has always been key to knowing God, discovering His paths and living in His favor.

"Beyond 2020, the future gets easier, not harder!"

In order to live in the rest of God you have to embrace the peace of God. The two are closely knit together.

The peace of God is a state of mind or being, whereas the rest of God is the result of taking on the mind of Christ, which leads us into this ultimate place of resting in Him.

The Promise Land

In Old Testament times, entering into the *"Promised Land"* was a picture of God leading His people into a place of rest.

The *"Sabbath Day"* in Old Testament scripture was a type and shadow of "Jesus Christ" who was destined to become our final place of rest. In this sense, the *"Sabbath Day"* is not a day, but a person, named Jesus.

The Promised Land is not a future location in time, but a person named, Jesus.

The Hebrew word *"Shalom"* refers to *"an inward sense of peace, completeness, wholeness or tranquility.* In Israel, when people greet each other or say goodbye, they often use the word, *"Shalom.* "Its implications are, *"May you be full of well-being" or "full health and prosperity be upon you."*

However, *"Shalom"* also describes the *"absence of war."*

This profoundly highlights the previous chapter, ***"No More War!"***

As already stated, even though there's evidence of spiritual conflict all around us, we don't have to become victims of a conflicted mind, but instead living as **more than conquerors** in Him.

"So now I live with the confidence that there is nothing in the universe with the power to separate us from God's love. I'm convinced that his love will triumph over death, life's troubles, fallen angels, or dark rulers in the heavens. There is nothing in our present or future circumstances that can weaken his love. There is no power above us or beneath us—no power that could ever be found in the universe that can distance us from God's passionate love, which is lavished upon us through our Lord Jesus, the Anointed One!"
(Romans 8:38-39 TPT)

I must reiterate, as long as we allow ourselves to be dominated by *a "warfare mentality"* we cannot expect to see the supernatural rest and peace of God. The two contradict each other.

Speaking to David, God said:

"Behold, a son will be born to you, who shall be a man of rest; and I will give him rest from all his enemies on every side; for his name shall be Solomon and I will give peace and quiet to Israel in his days.
(1 Chronicles 22:9)

Jesus declared:

"I leave the gift of peace with you—my peace. Not the kind of fragile peace given by the world, but my perfect peace. Don't yield to fear or be troubled in your hearts—instead, be courageous!
(John 14:27 TPT)

I love the idea Jesus left His peace with us. I also love His peace is supernatural, unlike the peace of the world, which is circumstantial. This is the good news!

Entering His Rest

The Hebrew word for rest is *"nuach"* which means: *"to rest or to be quiet."* Sometimes, it is synonymous to *"shabat"* which means to cease or to rest. The Greek word for *"rest"* is *"refreshment."* In this sense, ***"refreshing comes from the presence of the Lord."***

"And now you must repent and turn back to God so that your sins will be removed, and so that times of refreshing, will stream from the Lord's presence. And he will send you Jesus, the Messiah, the chosen one for you. For he must remain in heaven until the restoration

of all things, has taken place, fulfilling everything that God said long ago through his holy prophets."
(Acts 3:19-21 TPT)

The future is about an age of repentance, at which time the people of God return home, back to the revelation of God's love. This is when God's people enter into the revelation the law of sin and death has been obliterated from their lives.

Having said that, beyond 2020 we will see generations moving past a repenting mindset, into a kingdom revelation of what it means to rest in God, which is a place of faith and trust.

The word *"refreshing"* is in reference to the breath of God, which depicts the *"ruach"* the *"wind or breath"* of God given to Adam in the Garden. As you can see, all of this and more, points to the *"universal restoration"* of all things.

Therefore we declare:

"We are in the age of the restoration of all things." This includes the restoration of all creation, not just humanity.

The revealing of this kingdom age of rest and peace is the final consummation, the end and the beginning of all things. It's the intent of Father for all creation.

The final declaration of Jesus Christ to enter into His rest was:

"...It is finished..."
(John 19:30)

In the book of Hebrews we discover one of the primary barriers to entering into the rest of God is unbelief.

"It is clear they could not enter into their inheritance because they wrapped their hearts in unbelief." (Hebrews 3:19 TPT)

This means a restful generation of believers will display a level of love, faith and power the world is waiting to witness.

Again, the emphasis to enter His rest is undeniable:

"For those of us who believe, faith activates the promise and we experience the realm of confident rest! For he has said, "I was grieved with them and made a solemn oath, 'They will never enter into the calming rest of my Spirit.' "God's works have all been completed from the foundation of the world. "For it says in the Scriptures, "On the seventh day God rested from all his works." And again, as stated before, "They will never enter into my calming place of rest." (Hebrews 4:3-5 TPT)

First, notice how the rest of God is described as a ***"realm of confident rest."***

It seems the primary grievance God had with ancient Israel was lacking the confidence in His intentions toward them, which prevented them from entering into a supernatural realm of intimate faith.

We often hear about the "law of attraction."

From a spiritual perspective, I've discovered the law of attraction is a realm of faith and confidence in God, which attracts the supernatural favor of God in my life. This same spiritual reality is generating an unfathomable love for His people.

Every amazing thing I share in this book is a supernatural by-product of walking out on the plank of faith and taking the plunge into endless possibilities.

It's important to see God was inviting Israel into the works of heaven, which were completed before the foundations of the world. In other words, the same rest God entered into after creating all things was offered to Israel in their day. Wow!

Of course, we know now, this place of rest is none other than the revelation of sonship, which is the Word, who became Jesus, the manifested Son of God.

The conclusion of God's restful and peaceful intent brings us to this final summary.

Now if this promise of "rest" was fulfilled when Joshua brought the people into the land, God wouldn't have spoken later of another "rest" yet to come. So we conclude that there is still a full and complete "rest" waiting for believers to experience .As we enter into God's faith-rest life we cease from our own works, just as God celebrates his finished works and rests in them. So then we must give our all and be eager to experience this faith-rest life, so that no one falls short by following the same pattern of doubt and unbelief.
(Hebrews 4:8-11)

If you are wondering what the future looks like, this is it. It looks like the realm of rest and peace coming upon the Earth as in heaven. It looks like a sea of faith covering the Earth. It reveals a *"faith-rest life"* with eternal patterns of love and glory. This will become the ultimate invitation of the final appearing of Jesus, thus the merging of Heaven and Earth.

Historical Repetitions

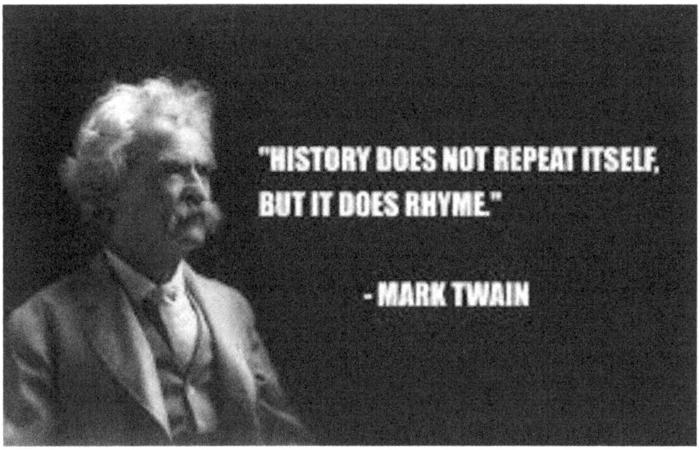

It is said that Mark Twain once commented:

"History doesn't repeat itself, but it often rhymes."

I would like to take this a step further and say:

"The idea of history repeating itself is over."

Beyond 2020, multiple generations will realize they are not just a cycling process of life, but a unique, one of a kind, eternal glory, born out of the love of God.

It will soon become very evident the body of Christ, and the world, is breaking out of ancient repetitive patterns of history. The idea of history repeating itself will soon become a thing of the past.

We will then see more clearly what it means to go from glory to glory.

"We can all draw close to him with the veil removed from our faces. And with no veil we all become like mirrors who brightly reflect the glory of the Lord Jesus. We are being transfigured into his very image

as we move from one brighter level of glory to another. And this glorious transfiguration comes from the Lord, who is the Spirit." (2 Corinthians 3:18 TPT)

Beyond 2020 will be the age of total transparency. It will be the age of unveiling the wisdom and knowledge of God's love beyond any former comprehension. It will be the age of reflecting glory of Jesus for all eternity. It will be the age of a glorious transfiguration of the body of Christ, and all creation.

In this sense, I announce to you today:

"We are breaking free from an historical repetitive cycle of life. We are moving beyond a mindset that has held the people of God hostage to a repetitious mentality."

We are advancing toward our fullest potential in the kingdom of God. We are breaking free from any former restraint.

There's a difference between spiraling up the mountain of the Lord versus just going around and around, only to meet at the same starting point. God never intended for His people to live a merry-go-round life. Because of disobedience, Israel wandered around in the wilderness for forty years.

"The age of wandering aimlessly through life is over."

Beyond 2020, we will witness the disappearance of any repetitive pattern outside the government of God's love.

As another divine layer of glory covers the Earth, the illusion of time and space between heaven and Earth will incrementally disappear. Hence the reality of the kingdom of God; the kingdom of heaven, will become extremely apparent.

Unfortunately, many still believe we are going from darkness to darkness, rather than glory to glory. This illusion of darkness is about to be profoundly interrupted.

Beyond 2020, we will emphatically mark an intense transformative age and restoration of all things. This is inclusive to **"the great awakening"** not just for humanity, but also for all creation.

No Going Back

For years, I have prophetically declared:

"As a nation, as sons and daughters of God, we will never go back to our former state of captivity."

Many find it hard to believe when I say:

"The United States will never go back to its former decayed state of government."

This same word holds true for other nations in the world. As they continue to rise out of the ashes of death, they will never return to their former state of darkness. Come on God!

Again Paul writes:

"Now, if anyone is enfolded into Christ, he has become an entirely new creation. All that is related to the old order has vanished. Behold, everything is fresh and new."
(2 Corinthians 5:17 TPT)

The word ***"vanished"*** in this text is defined as:

"Our old identity, our life of sin, the power of Satan, the religious works of trying to please God, our old relationship with the world, and our old mind-sets. We are not reformed or simply refurbished, we are made completely new by our union with Christ and the indwelling of the Holy Spirit."

This definition points to the unfolding revelation of a supernatural life style in the kingdom of God. It's the unveiling of the divine order of heaven.

Let's take a moment and step into agreement with the intentions of heaven by prophetically declaring these words:

"I'm not going back! We are not going back to what used to be! The old me, before Christ, has completely vanished away!"

Let's take it a step further by being a little more specific as to the life we are ***not*** going back to.

- **I am not going back to any previous form of decay.**
- **I am not going back to any old way of thinking.**
- **I am not going back to lack.**
- **I am not going back to debt.**
- **I am not going back to any previous sickness or disease.**
- **I am not going back to unhealthy relationships.**
- **I am not going back to a life of fear.**

I am not going back!

Paul writes:

"...I forget all of the past as I fasten my heart to the future instead. I run straight for the divine invitation of reaching the heavenly goal and gaining the victory-prize through the anointing of Jesus." (Philippians 3:13-14 TPT)

I realize there are some actions in life worth repeating, but each repetitive moment should be done at a higher level of relationship and understanding in the kingdom of God.

Governmental Flip

The prophetic word I'm about to share with you was confirmed though an amazing sign and wonder in space. It was as if God was making sure everyone in the world had a front row seat to its affirmation.

I first released this word as an article, and the next day as a podcast. During the podcast, I told the audience I could hear the sound of **Flipper.**

At the end of this prophet word, I will share with you the song and the final declaration I spoke over those listening.

So before I share how this prophetic word was amazingly confirmed in the heavens, let me share with you the article I had written a week or so prior to its affirmation.

It reads:

"God is so creative and has an amazing sense of humor. I recently saw an image of "Flipper" (1964 TV series about a dolphin) while meditating on the future intent of God for this nation and the world.

Countless people are about to witness a major flip in their lives. This includes the United States government and other governments across the world.

The generals of technology are about to come face-to-face with a major flip in the world of communications. Many of the corporate giants today will move to the end of the food chain."

While reaching important goals in our life can be very rewarding, I think it's important to do so with the heart of God in mind.

For those who have chosen the path of honor and integrity, you can expect a major increase into the purposes of God for your life.

Beyond 2020, major governmental walls of obstruction are about to come down creating a glorious highway for kingdom of righteousness to rise on the Earth.

When Jesus entered the temple of Jerusalem and saw it was being used for personal gain, out of a righteous anger, He flipped over the tables of disrespect and defilement and drove the people out.

Immediately thereafter, He spoke these words:

"...It is written, my house shall be called a house of prayer..."
(Matthew 21:13)

Seemingly, in a moment, what once looked like a governmental take over in the temple of God was immediately brought into divine order.

You can be certain, outside of prophetic foresight, no one saw this unannounced man named Jesus coming.

I believe we have entered into another display of witnessing another unannounced governmental take over. This is not just in reference to the United States, but multiple governments worldwide.

The word *"flip"* is defined as, *"causing something to turn over with a sudden sharp move."*

"I see a sharp turn ahead!" As you might guess, sharp turns are often very challenging. Anyone who fails to see the warning signs in advance can become vulnerable to an unexpected *"flip!"*

As the government of this nation, and the world, make another turn into the intent of heaven on Earth, governmental leaders will suddenly begin flipping across all parties of government.

Those who were once viewed as enemies of God will unexpectedly flip over to the other side of agreement with righteousness.

It reminds me of Saul in the New Testament, who was once perceived as an enemy of God, but through divine intervention his perspective of government, was suddenly flipped into a new field of righteous understanding.

Again, outside of any prophetic foresight, no one saw this coming.

"I have long said, "The government of this nation will never go back to what it was before. I still stand on that word today."

Don't be sucked into any negative illusion of the current state of government in the world.

"I believe an unusual flipping of the House is just around the corner."

Many think the recent election of the house of congress in the United States is an irreversible event. Let me assure you; it will prove to be quite the opposite.

As already mentioned,

"An unexpected crossing of the isle of government in favor of righteousness will soon come into view."

A greater dissatisfaction is beginning to form within the Democratic party of this nation and its true displeasure will eventually come into maturity in 2020.

However, even before 2020 comes into play, I have a sense some key people of government will flip their position on important issues that pertain to the righteous progression of this nation and the world.

I am presently being reminded of a prophetic word the Lord spoke to me on January 12, 2011.

"Another step will be added to the government of the United States."

I'm not pretending to know what **"another step"** really means, but I have an idea it points to another branch of government called "**Space Force**."

Many who read this will become supernaturally impregnated with a governmental flip in your life for 2020.

Some of you feel like you are being backed into a corner of defeat, but I want to prophetically announce to you today:

"God did not bring you this far to leave you behind. Whether you are wrestling with guilt, shame, despair, sickness or any other voidance of life, God has your back. Maybe you feel you have been limited to a narrowing stream of living water, but God is about to plunge you into the ocean of plenty."

Here are the Flipper lyrics:

"They call him Flipper, Flipper, faster than lightning, No-one you see, is smarter than he. And we know Flipper, Flipper, lives in a world full of wonder, flying there-under, under the sea!"

After singing this song, over the air, I declared these words on the podcast:

"In a moment, faster than lightning, many of you are going to discover the genius of heaven in you. God is about to flip you into a world full of awe and wonder, where you will discover the endless oceans of God's love and glory! Come on God!"

On the heels of releasing this article and podcast, NASA discovered this unusual photo of a dolphin on Jupiter. Though the image was captured mid November 2018, it took a few weeks before the image was actually discovered and released to the public.

On November 12, 2018 NASA reports: NASA captured a new image of a cosmic "dolphin" formation within Jupiter's clouds.

Come on God! This is amazing! God painted a dolphin on Jupiter to let you know He is about to flip our world upside down!

Future Kingdom Economics

While writing this book, I heard a recent report of a possible recession hitting the United States. On the heels of that national economical prediction, these words rose up in my spirit:

"The age of recession is over. The United States will never see recession again."

My heart leapt with a resounding, *"Yes Lord!"*

Beyond 2020, I believe the United States and parts of the world, will step over the threshold of present economics into a world of economical brilliance. Mind you, this brilliance will far surpass the natural realm. Every day the kingdom of the world is being engulfed by the kingdom of glory.

Under the leadership of Donald Trump we have witnessed a major financial boost in the United States. In many ways this nation has taken a giant step toward the purposes and intent of God for His people.

Prior to this time many were convinced we were on our way down; destined to become beggars at the porches of other nations.

The sudden shift toward an increasing economy has left many in a world of dusty bewilderment. They are still in disbelief of our current progression toward a brighter future.

Of course, all the above coincides with the previous chapter *"End of Historic Repetitions."*

"We will never go back again! We will never go back to a life of captivity! We will never go back into darkness! We will never go back to less than the intended purpose of God for our lives!"

It's important to remember, we are not predicting the future, but co-creating the future intent of God for His people.

This creative realm of glory is the new bold frontier of endless possibilities

In 2001, during one of our early prophetic gatherings at ***Mountain Top International*** in Yakima, Washington, I had an open vision of a barren land that looked completely void of any life. It reminded me of an empty waterless desert. During this encounter, God spoke to me and said:

"I am giving you this barren land as a canvas of opportunity to co-create with me. Prophesy my future expectations for my people and you will witness a well of new life springing up in the desert."

I was instantly reminded of God inviting Ezekiel to co-create with Him. He showed Ezekiel a valley of dry bones, a lifeless nation (Israel) in a dry and thirsty land. But as soon as Ezekiel began to prophesy over this barren people called, "Israel" he saw by the spirit, an entire nation coming back to life.

"The hand of the Lord was upon me, and He brought me out by the Spirit of the Lord and set me down in the middle of the valley; and it was full of bones. He caused me to pass among them round about, and behold, there were very many on the surface of the valley; and lo, they

were very dry. He said to me, "Son of man, can these bones live?" And I answered, "O Lord God, You know." Again He said to me, "Prophesy over these bones and say to them, 'O dry bones, hear the word of the Lord.' Thus says the Lord God to these bones, 'Behold, I will cause breath to enter you that you may come to life. I will put sinews on you, make flesh grow back on you, cover you with skin and put breath in you that you may come alive; and you will know that I am the Lord." (Ezekiel 37:1-10)

Ezekiel continued to describe how the bones and flesh came together. Then through prophetic utterance, Ezekiel spoke to the four winds commanding the breath of God to fill the nation of Israel, bringing it to its feet. What an amazing historical account of a co-creative moment with God.

This was my first introduction on how to live and function, beyond the office of a prophet, into the revelation of sonship, as a co-creator of heaven on Earth.

"Beyond 2020, I see an army of people in the kingdom of God shifting out of a beggar's mentality into the revelation of sonship. I see lovers of God commanding the Earth to align itself with the heart and mind of God. I see a generation of sons and daughters co-creating at a much higher level than Ezekiel did in his day."

Come on! Ezekiel is saying, "You've got this! You can do this! All heaven is celebrating your supernatural advancement in the kingdom of God."

Our only recourse is to go into the revelation of our eternal glory in God's kingdom and behold our true state, our true life in the love of our Father. One glimpse of His endless love and glory will wreck us forever.

The age of acceleration is upon us. This means the prophetic declarations of the people of God will come into view within moments, days, and weeks.

I've come to realize the more I live in the future; the more present the future lives in me.

I believe this is the key to seeing the gap between today and tomorrow narrowing down into a present glory no longer governed by time and space.

I am often saddened by the perceptions of numerous prophets who seem to be mesmerized by future evil. I remember reading an excerpt from Shawn Bolz:

"We aren't called to discern evil as a goal, we are called to discern God's heart. That means sometimes we will see evil so we can see what God wants to do about it." (Shawn Bolz/Translating God)

I love this perspective. It's not denying evil things happen, but it's seeing evil from the perspective of God's heart, thus releasing the solutions of heaven on Earth.

It's time for the church to come out of prophetic generalizations (shadows and types) of future outcomes, and offer specific hopeful solutions for a greater tomorrow.

I am a strong believer the economics of heaven are within our grasp. This means the economics of the world are within our jurisdiction as well.

Over the years, I have continued to move beyond the door of an endless revelation of the goodness of God. As a result, I've learned to co-create with God on many different levels.

In 2010, I prophetically spoke:

"A new currency would come into view, one that would break the barrier of a lessor value, which would make way for an historic economical breakthrough"

During our New Year's Eve gathering on December 31, 2016, I declared:

"The standard financial value of currency in the business world, would no longer be gauged by thousands or millions, but would shift from billions to trillions, and the aftermath of this enormous financial shift would create a new floor and ceiling for future financial corporations."

I saw the present value of the US currency, suddenly blast upward like a rocket. I watched by the spirit as it broke through ancient walls.

This word was released during the wake of a hopeless economical time in the United States.

On August 2, 2018 CNBC reported:

"Apple hit a market cap of $1 trillion on Thursday — and hung onto the record valuation at market close — as the iPhone maker became the first publicly traded U.S. company to reach $1 trillion."

On September 4, 2018, the Washington Post announced, "Amazon joined the trillion-dollar rank."

"Amazon.com on Tuesday became the second publicly traded U.S. Company to be valued at more than $1 trillion, as the tech giant expands into new lines of business that are helping turn record profits."

Currently, the entire world is in the midst of a global economic shift. The United States is shifting from its former dependency on other countries for its resources to creating its own. This is not to say we won't continue to trade with other nations, but it does mean we will no longer be at the mercy of those who would otherwise try to take advantage of their positions of power.

David writes:

"I have been young and now I am old, yet I have not seen the

righteous forsaken or his descendants begging bread. All day long he is gracious and lends, and his descendants are a blessing." (Psalms 37:25-26)

Beyond 2020, the world will be struck with the realization God truly does favor righteousness.

Most believe the future economics of our nation, and the world is largely determined by the repetitive behavior of humanity. As a nation, the idea of being trillions of dollars in debt is very unnerving.

Here's another bold creative moment:

"The Lord has shown me; by 2024 the United States will become virtually debt free. Come on God!"

As sons and daughters of God, our perspective of the future should always be based on the endless supply of heaven. Seeing the future from any other view can potentially reduce our ability to walk in true abundance.

As a people in God, we are empowered to lay hold of the riches of heaven and release them on the Earth.

Again, the future economy is not from below, but from above. In this sense, we are standing on the edge of an entirely new economical threshold. This economy doesn't just rely on the present limited genius of humanity, but on a new field of genius and creativity. It will have the ability to redefine, and yes, even reinvent the wheel for future economical potentials.

The stock markets operate much like an auction house. They enable buyers and sellers to negotiate prices and make trades.

In turn, Investors then buy and sell these stocks amongst themselves, and the stock exchange tracks the supply and demand of each listed stock. At the end of the day, most of all the above is based on ***future potentials and expectations.***

Potential Expectations

Beyond 2020, we will witness a major shift in potential expectations. Potential is descriptive of something possible, but not yet visible. In terms of the kingdom of God,

"...All things are possible to him who believes."
(Mark 9:23)

Potential refers to the capacity to grow into the greater you.

"Faith is the assurance *(creative force)* ***of things hoped for,*** *(the potential)* ***the conviction*** *(outcome)* ***of things not seen."***
(Hebrews 11:1)

Secondly, *"expectation"* is, *"The hope of what you are currently seeing in the present has the potential to become something greater in the future."*

All the above should lead us into the amazing realization the future economics of the entire world hinges on our ability to see beyond the current existence of the natural realm, into the invisible potential of an expectant economy not yet visible.

No matter how great something might appear in the moment, it has the potential to become even greater in the future.

We can either align ourselves with a limited earthly economy or synchronize ourselves to the highest economics of heaven. Ultimately, we must never forget:

The greatest economy of heaven is not measured in dollars and cents, but in the depths of God's love.

The natural fruit of the land is part of our inheritance in the kingdom of God.

An Angel Named Outlander

In October 15, 2017, Tamera and I flew to Seoul, South Korea to speak at a conference in the city of Daejeon. Prior to our meeting times, I made a video titled, "Supernatural Invites." I reemphasized the importance of engaging with creation and inviting creation to respond to the glory of God in us.

During our first meeting that night at Jesus Glory Church, my eyes were opened to the realm of the Spirit. At which time, I saw an angel in the cosmos, kneeling down before a stack of colorful blocks, which looked like children blocks, about 3'x 3' in size.

The angel appeared to be very focused, as if seeing something I was not aware of. There were titles inscribed on the face of each block in front of him. One block in particular caught my eye. The name ***"Uncommon"*** was written across the face of it.

As soon as I read this title, I had knowledge the Angel's name was Outlander. To be honest, I was taken back by the thought there was actually an angel named Outlander. It sounded like something out of

Hollywood.

I was suddenly jarred out of this encounter by the pastor announcing my name; inviting me to come up and speak. As you can imagine, my heart and mind was still reeling in what had just happened. As I began to speak, a spirit of spontaneous revelation overcame me.

"I believe we are about to witness an outlandish event in the outer limits of space, all of which will be witnessed by the entire world."

As I continue to prophetically speak about future outcomes, I knew I was functioning from a place of co-creating with God.

However, I couldn't help but think how foolish I probably looked to Outlander. Me, not knowing he had been with me all these years. This had to be somewhat humorous and frustrating for him. Anyone who is aware of my life and journey in God would understand why I would feel this way. Over the years, I have witnessed many outlandish events on Earth, and in the heavens above. In addition, I've always believed learning how to work with our angels is vitally important to the progression of our life and destiny in God.

Oh well, as the saying goes, *"live and learn."*

As I continued to speak, I felt impressed to quickly look up the word *"Uncommon."* It's defined as, *"rare, outlandish, historic or unusual, etc...."* **(Merriam-Webster Dictionary)**

What? No way! Uncommon is in reference to outlandish events, hence, the name Outlander. Seemingly, all in one swift moment, everything came together. It was as though another layer of glory had come over me. I knew my life would never be the same.

The very next day, Tamera and I were at the hotel having our morning coffee, when a **Foxnews** alert appeared on my phone.

It read:

"Astronomers Strike Gravitational Gold In Colliding Neutron Stars." ***(Robin Dienel/Carnegie Institution for Science)***

The article went on say, on October 16, 2017 NASA and The World of Physicists and Astronomers released and astounding report of two neutron stars historically colliding together.

Other reports told how the collision of these two neutron stars resulted in an unfathomable amount of gold, platinum, silver and other metals being spewed out all over space.

If you take the time to Google this event you will discover some other crazy and fascinating information connected to this galactic phenomenon. The wild thing was this neutron collision actually took place130 million years prior, but given how many light years away this event was, it didn't show up until now. Wow!

When we returned to the morning session of the conference, we shared the amazing news. You could feel the atmosphere shift into a crazy realm of wild faith. It had the presence of sonship.

Beyond 2020, we will witness the most outlandish events ever witnessed before, both on Earth and in the heavens above. I also believe we are coming into a divine partnership with angels at a level the Ekklesia has ever witnessed.

This is but another example of the greatest awakening the world has ever seen cover the Earth as the waters cover the sea.

The Age Of Awareness

The lack of awareness can often make us vulnerable to hazardous potentials. It's so easy to become distracted by the everyday activities in life. In our business, we often fail to recognize any impending dangers that might be lurking.

Beyond 2020, the influence of God's kingdom rises to its expected influence in the world, we will continually see the evils of humanity appear in horrible ways.

I'm not implying we walk around with a fearful or suspicious mind. However, in light of the current potentials of evil in the world, it would serve us well to develop our spiritual sensory.

Rest assured, regardless of any future outbursts of violence, the people of God are maturing into their supernatural inheritance in the kingdom of God. As a result, we will increasingly run interference in the face of every evil intention of the enemy.

Recently, while writing this book another mass shooting unfolded, back-to-back, in El Paso, Texas and Dayton, Ohio. These horrific events took the lives of 31 people and dozens of others were injured.

These horrendous acts of violence are always deeply disturbing to me. I know many of you reading this feel the same. Not only do I feel a deep sadness for those who have lost loved ones in such a violent way, but I also feel angry I wasn't able to somehow keep it from happening.

I know some of you are thinking; how could I or anyone else have prevented something like this from happening?

Supernatural Interventions

Not only are we entering deeper into an age of supernatural awareness, but also into an age of glorious intervention.

For some time now, I have personally developed and walked in a greater realm of spiritual awareness; as a result, I've engaged with a greater realm of *"glorious intervention."*

During one of my earlier travels to Israel, my daughter Amber and a few others joined me. During our visit, I told everyone with me, *"I have only one important request, if for any reason I sense an urgency to leave an area at any given time; you have to agree to leave with me without question."* They agreed.

At the time of our visit, there were still some heated issues taking place at the Gaza border.

While none of us felt fearful, we were a bit cautious. A few days into our visit we decided to travel to Bethlehem then make our way toward Jericho.

We first visited a few historical sights, before venturing into the market place. My daughter Amber, like her mother, loves to shop. Both her and her mother had the ability to miraculously disappear in any given store, regardless of its size.

After about an hour or so, I suddenly had this urgency rise up within me. It had the feel of a panic attack, but I knew it was God sounding a cautionary alarm in my spirit.

I immediately called everyone on my cell to meet me at the entrance of the market. However, Amber was not answering her phone. Surprise!

I hurriedly searched through the market place, being careful not to transmit any kind of panic. Within a few minutes I finally found Amber. As you might have guessed, my urgency wasn't necessarily hers. She responded with, "Seriously dad, I was just getting into some good shopping." "Come on Amber, you promised, "I replied.

After our departure, we continued on to Jericho and a few other places before heading back to the home where we were staying with a close friend.

That same evening we heard on the news someone had stabbed and killed a young Jewish boy in the Bethlehem market place where we were earlier that day. The stabbing resulted in a major outburst of violence and many more were seriously injured.

When we heard the news, we shockingly looked at each other realizing, when God breaks through everything is subject to change.

Beyond 2020, we will witness divine interventions to such degree; thousands upon thousands of people will be spared the horrid actions of a murdering spirit. Amazing supernatural displays of unnatural boldness will stop bullets of death as if they were mimicking some Hollywood display of the Matrix.

The Elisha Connection

Being connected to the heart and mind of God is obviously very important. Being in tune with His voice is equally important. While there are several instances in the Bible that reveal a type of supernatural awareness and intervention, one of my favorites is that of Elisha:

"When the king of Aram was at war with Israel, he would confer with his officers and say, "We will mobilize our forces at such and such a place. "But immediately Elisha, the man of God, would warn the king of Israel, "Do not go near that place, for the Arameans are planning to mobilize their troops there." So the king of Israel would send word to the place indicated by the man of God. Time and again Elisha warned the king, so that he would be on the alert there .The king of Aram became very upset over this. He called his officers together and demanded, "Which of you is the traitor? Who has been informing the king of Israel of my plans? "It's not us, my lord the king," one of the officers replied. "Elisha, the prophet in Israel, tells the king of Israel even the words you speak in the privacy of your bedroom!"
(2 Kings 6:18-13 NLT)

As you can see, Elisha's warnings of Aram's plan's to attack Israel served as a huge connection to God, thus a continual intervention to the King of Israel. This degree of insight is not just limited to a prophetic mantle, but is available to anyone who has an intimate walk with God.

"God wants to reveal the intentions of the enemy more than we want to know them. He is looking for anyone who is willing to listen."

Beyond 2020, this kind of kingdom awareness and preventive power against the acts of evil will become a common practice throughout the world.

Imagine plans of mass murder and countless other acts of evil being made known before they have the opportunity to take the life of innocent men, women and children.

These supernatural interventions are happening right now, many of which are coming through spiritual discernment, the gift of knowledge, dreams, visions etc.

All of these powerful avenues of divine interventions have even joined themselves to the presidency of Donald Trump, and other key men and women in government. Many of who carry the righteous intent of heaven on Earth.

Beyond 2020, we will witness a global connection of God with His people that will exceed any technology, including the Internet.

There is no greater source of knowledge than being directly connected to the heart and mind of God for His people.

This divine connection has ability to exceed any technology in the world. It has the ability to know the plans of God, as well as the plans of the enemy.

In 2020, we will witness an internet of glory. A web of heavenly insight and foresight will exceed the reach of the *"dark web"* of knowledge and information currently trying to invade every home in the world.

Right now, I am revealing to you an extraordinary future exposure and divine intervention that will result in the collapse of a global technical giant. It has secretly given itself over to a spirit of control, with the intentions to undermine the increase of heaven on Earth.

The Waves of Ireland

For over a decade, I have publicly witnessed some crazy responses of creation to the sonship of God in me, and His people. All were undeniable fulfillments and reactions to the prophetic word of God.

Around the fall of 2011, I was in the town of Bray, County Wicklow, Ireland when I released a prophetic word about historic waves rising in the ocean waters of that region. I prophetically spoke how this event would be followed by new exports. I also spoke about the city of Bray celebrating gold in the near future.

During that prophetic moment, I began to describe to the people the historic waves I could see crashing down on the shores of their coastal region. In the spirit, I could literally feel creation responding to the Word of God coming out of me. It felt as though everything was being aligned for future fulfillment. I will never forget the sensation I felt as I walked on top of the waves of the ocean that were destined to hit the coast of Northern Ireland.

I wondered, *"Was this what Jesus felt in His day when He walked on the waters in the midst of the storm?"*

Afterwards, I remember walking out of the meeting that night with my longtime friend Josh Crofton. We were both extremely impacted by what had just happened. We started nervously joking about getting on the plane before the great storm hit.

We both knew it was not a storm of devastation, but a storm of future manifestations that would capture the hearts of God's people.

A couple days later, after landing back home in the United States, the pastors from the local church in Bray, County Wicklow, sent me an email about a sudden storm hitting their coastal waters; creating historic high waves. The historic waves were the *first* portion of the prophetic declaration released in Bray.

The *second* portion of prophecy spoke about new exports coming out of Ireland.

Not too long after, Ireland discovered a huge deposit of natural gas, and for the first time ever, became an exporter of this new found treasure.

The *third* portion of the prophecy spoke about the city of Bray celebrating Gold.

In 2012, during the winter Olympic Games in London, Olympian, Katie Taylor won Ireland's **first gold medal**. She was from Bray, County Wicklow, Ireland. After this historic win, Katie and her caravan of Olympic supporters paraded down the streets of Bray, while thousands celebrated her golden victory.

Wow! Come on God! Even as I share this glorious word with you, I have a strong sense in my spirit, 2020, and beyond, will reveal in you a celebration of kingdom advancement.

Now, I can see a cloud witnesses celebrating the gold you have purchased with your faith in God. This is nothing less than the refiners gold, Peter and John write about in their day.

"May the thought of this cause you to jump for joy, even though lately you've had to put up with the grief of many trials. But these only reveal the sterling core of your faith, which is far more valuable than gold that perishes, for even gold is refined by fire. Your authentic faith will result in even more praise, glory, and honor when Jesus the Anointed One is revealed."
(1 Peter 1:6-7 TPT)

John writes:

"So I counsel you to purchase gold perfected by fire, so that you can be truly rich. Purchase a white garment to cover and clothe your shameful Adam-nakedness. Purchase eye salve to be placed over your eyes so that you can truly see."
(Revelation 3:18 TPT)

This kingdom gold of glory is nothing less than the love of Jesus paying the price for you and me to come into the revelation of being sons and daughters of God. We purchase this redeeming glory through our faith and commitment to life and purposes of God for His people.

Beyond 2020, we will witness the **golden ages of God's** kingdom. At which time, the garments of righteousness that have been given to us through the blood of Jesus, will be displayed with great purpose and intent in all the kingdoms of the world. Come on God!

The Kingdom Trumpet

"Then the seventh angel sounded his trumpet, and a loud voice broke forth in heaven, saying: "The kingdom of the world has become the kingdom of our God and of his Anointed One! He will reign supreme for an eternity of eternities!"
(Revelation 11:15 TPT)

The kingdom of God is swallowing up the kingdom of this world.

The word *"world"* is also defined as: *"The kingdom of finance, culture and government; religious and secular."*

All the above is the revelation of every kingdom in the world coming under the dominion of God's love, glory and power.

I want to reemphasize the importance of seeing the world from the perspective of God's love and glory invading the Earth.

The last trumpet, which is being trumpeted right now, is not about some end time demise of humanity, but the sound of the world being transferred under the ruler ship of heaven.

It's the sound of the supremacy of the ***"Anointed One"*** declaring the finished work of His kingdom for all eternity.

It's imperative we train our spiritual senses to perceive heavenly matters. I'm continually discovering a supernatural world of living that exceeds anything I could've ever hoped for or imagine.

Right when I think I have plateaued on God's eternal plan for humanity, or myself, I soon discover another ancient pathway leading deeper into the Father's heart.

Many end time philosophers never dreamed the United States, and other nations in the world, would ever turn the corner from its previous darkened state. But here we are standing on the threshold of divine intervention where we will witness the glory of God's kingdom flooding the Earth.

On the surface there are still extreme acts of violence, expressed hatred and division, but underneath there's a rumbling sound of glory that's about to erupt into the last trumpeting sound of the peace and rest of God.

Regardless of any apparent increase of heaven on Earth, many still refuse to embrace a hopeful tomorrow. They are gripped with the idea a hopeful outcome for any nation is empty and void of any future hope.

As Jesus drew closer to His appointment with death and the grave, He:

"...Who for the joy set before Him endured the cross..."
(Hebrews 12:2)

Another translation reads:

"...Because his heart was focused on the joy of knowing that you would be his, he endured the agony of the cross and conquered its humiliation, and now sits exalted at the right hand of the throne of God!"
(Hebrews 12:2 TPT)

I believe this amazing joyful perspective of Jesus was twofold. First, seeing we would be joined together with the Father. Secondly, Jesus seeing Himself reunited with His Father in glory.

Thus the words of Jesus:

"Now, Father, glorify Me together with Yourself, with the glory which I had with You before the world was."
(John 17:5)

Beyond 2020, while the enemy continues to stir up future formulas of death and decay, a glorious display of abundant life is about to erupt upon the face of the Earth, overtaking the hearts of billions of people.

The Gates Of Heaven Are Open

"Lift up your heads, O gates, and be lifted up, O ancient (everlasting) doors, that the King of glory may come in! Who is the King of glory? The Lord strong and mighty; the Lord mighty in battle. Lift up your heads, O gates, and lift them up, O ancient doors, that the King of glory may come in! Who is this King of glory? The Lord of hosts, He is the King of glory."
(Psalms 24:7-10)

Beyond 2020, the revelation of being an open gate of heaven on Earth will be greater realized. The idea is to first lift up our heads, which corresponds with the words of

Paul when he wrote:

"Set your mind on the things above, not on the things that are on earth."
(Colossians 3:2)

"Setting your mind" refers to *"setting your attention on God's glory,"* thus having your thoughts filled with heavenly realities.

Another translation reads:

"Yes, feast on all the treasures of the heavenly realm and fill your thoughts with heavenly realities, and not with the distractions of the natural realm."
(Colossians 3:2 TPT)

Once we turn our attention toward the heavenly realm, we are then lifted up into the treasures of God's glory. From there we are governmentally positioned to become everlasting doorways for the intent and purposes of God to be released upon the Earth.

These heavenly treasures include the supernatural insight and foresight of God's intentions for His people. This means, as co-creators with God, we are afforded the opportunity to prophetically release the government of heaven on Earth.

Again, this is a key to being enthroned in the heavenly realm. As we continue to live from the place of heaven, we become more aware as to the purpose of heaven on Earth. We continually live in the awareness we are releasing heaven by living in a place of glory, rather than, living in a place of darkness, waiting for the glory to come.

When living with an enthronement mentality the heavens are always open. Therefore, we don't have to pray for an open heaven, because we are an open heaven.

It's equally important we worship God from heaven down and not from Earth up. In this sense, every kingdom inspiration can extend our scepters of authority over the land, thus releasing the intent of Father over His people.

"Then I saw heaven opened, and suddenly a white horse appeared. The name of the one riding it was Faithful and True, and with pure righteousness he judges and rides to battle."
(Revelation 19:11 TPT)

When you recognize heaven is open, the white horse of justice will always appear. Faithfulness and truth will always reveal the purity of righteousness, which is the prevailing judgment over all things. Come on! Our God reigns!

The Age of Ascension

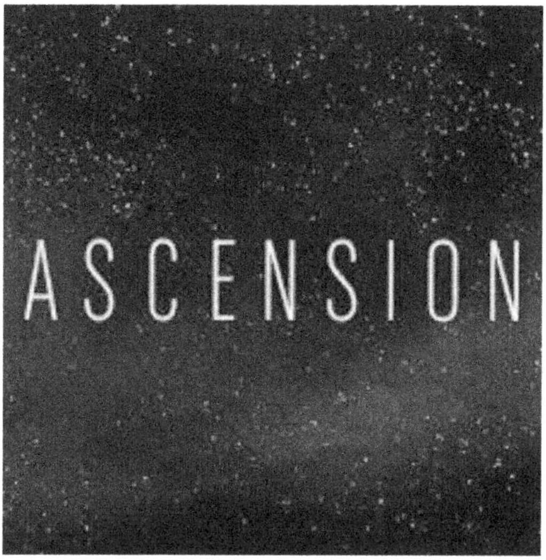

Beyond 2020, one will ascend, one will become extremely visible. This means the people of God are being elevated into the kingdom realms of heaven, thus the love, glory and power of God, greater than any other generation. This is the glory of the latter house exceeding the glory of the former.

"The latter glory of this house will be greater than the former,' says the Lord of hosts, 'and in this place I will give peace,' declares the Lord of hosts." (Haggai 2:9)

The glory of the Ekklesia is becoming more apparent, more visible throughout the world. As we enter deeper into our ascension in Jesus Christ, who is the doorway, the gateway of resurrection love and humility, we are able to access our divine inheritance in God at the level He desires us to.

Justin Paul Abraham, founder of **"Company of Burning Hearts"** describes repentance as: ***"The action of returning to our authentic origin in God."***

I love this! It reminds me of the book I wrote, ***"Total Recall, Remembering The Original You"*** which speaks about returning to the original authentic intent and design of Father's heart toward us.

The religious altar of repentance is being replaced by a daily turning of our hearts toward the love and knowledge of God given to us before time.

Speaking to Abraham, God declared:

"...Now lift up your eyes and look from the place where you are, northward and southward and eastward and westward; for all the land which you see, I will give it to you and to your descendants forever."
(Genesis 13:14-15)

Many have assumed Abraham was standing on a mountain with an awesome view in every direction. But God told Abraham to:

"...lift up your eyes and from the place where you are, all you can see is yours..."

The realm Abraham was standing in was nothing less than the mountain of the Lord, not in the Earth, but above the Earth.

This supernatural field of sight afforded Abraham the ability to see through time and space into the future promises of God.

We too, have access, in and on, the mountain of the Lord. As already stated, we are currently seated in heaven, in the heart of Father, which affords us the best view ever known to man.

From this place of heavenly ascension, like Abraham, we can see as far as the eyes of our heart can see. From our ascended state in glory we can see into our divine inheritance, which is waiting to be accessed now, not some day in the hereafter.

In heaven, there's a land that expresses the riches of the Father's heart so profoundly, they outweigh any wealth we could ever hope for or imagine. However, all the wealth of heaven, now and eternally, is living in us.

From our ascended state in glory, we are accessing future solutions for years to come. We are growing up into the knowledge of the Spirit, to such degree; a perishing spirit is being trampled under our feet.

As we ascend into our glorious state in the kingdom of God, the Earth expands having to make room for the increase of God's kingdom on Earth.

Every day is a continual invitation to come out of the old into the new. All of which, reveals in us the glory of God given to us before time.

A Timeless Generation

We are not looking or hoping for more time. As sons and daughters of God, we are co-creating with Father, therefore continually expanding the borders of time in heaven and on Earth.

No weapon formed against us will ever prosper because we have ascended above the threshold of darkness.

Because of ascended glory, the resurrection power of God's love in us, everything around us is being set free from the law of gravity. For years, I have spoken about the law of gravity being redefined. In the spirit, I have repeatedly seen the law of gravity, along with every other law of physics overridden with the weightlessness of eternal glory.

This means, on a spiritual level, every city, state and nation has the potential to be lifted up into an exalted state of glory.

"By the blessing of the upright a city is exalted, but by the mouth of the wicked it is torn down." (Proverbs 11:11)

You can be certain the blessing of the upright is without a doubt overriding the mouth of the wicked.

Ascended glory isn't just some kind of wave or move of God on Earth; it's the revelation of the bride of Christ being lifted up into her former perceived state of glory.

John describes it like this:

"Then in a vision I saw a new heaven and a new earth. The first heaven and earth had passed away, and the sea no longer existed. I saw the Holy City, the New Jerusalem, descending out of the heavenly realm from the presence of God, like a pleasing bride that had been prepared for her husband, adorned for her wedding. And I heard a thunderous voice from the throne, saying: "Look! God's tabernacle is with human beings. And from now on he will tabernacle with them as their God. Now God himself will have his home with them—'God-with-them' will be their God! He will wipe away every tear from their eye and eliminate death entirely. No one will mourn or weep any longer. The pain of wounds will no longer exist, for the old order has ceased. "And God-Enthroned spoke to me and said, "Consider this! I am making everything to be new and fresh. Write down at once all that I have told you, because each word is trustworthy and dependable." (Revelation 21:1-5 TPT)

Do you want to know what the future holds? This is it! You want to know how to create the future in accordance with the intentions of God for His people? This is it. This is the vision of Father for His future bride. This is the reason for our ascension into the glory of God.

It's for the purpose to bring all that is in heaven into the Earth. At such a time, a new heaven and a new Earth will be realized. All that used be will be no longer.

At the end of this age, we are the:

"Holy City, the New Jerusalem that descends out of the heavenly realm from the presence of God, appearing as a beautiful bride, adorned for our heavenly husband!"

Let's ascend so all that is in heaven, in us, in Christ, in the Father will descend upon the Earth for all eternity. At which time heaven and Earth will no longer be separated, but forever joined as one in God.

How To
Forget Unwanted
Memories
Michael A. Danforth

How To
Forget Unwanted
Memories
WORKBOOK
Michael A. Danforth

GUARDIANS
OF SPIRITUAL
MATURITY
Michael A. Danforth

next exit
TOTAL
RECALL
REMEMBERING THE
ORIGINAL YOU
AUTHOR
MICHAEL A. DANFORTH

Michael A. Danforth
God's Positive And Negative Equation
The Poetic Thread Of All Creation

SPACE
The Prophetic Frontier
Michael A. Danforth

68200131R00076

Made in the USA
Middletown, DE
21 September 2019